SEDUCED
BY A
SOCIOPATH

CHRISSY HANDY

WITH KATHRYN KNIGHT

HARPER
element

Certain details in this story, including names, places and dates, have been changed to protect privacy.

HarperElement
An imprint of HarperCollins*Publishers*
1 London Bridge Street
London SE1 9GF

www.harpercollins.co.uk

HarperCollins*Publishers*
1st Floor, Watermarque Building, Ringsend Road
Dublin 4, Ireland

First published by HarperElement 2022

1 3 5 7 9 10 8 6 4 2

A catalogue record of this book is
available from the British Library

PB ISBN 978-0-00-852227-8
TPB ISBN 978-0-00-852233-9

Printed and bound in the UK using 100%
renewable electricity at CPI Group (UK) Ltd

MIX
Paper from
responsible sources
FSC™ C007454

This book is produced from independently certified FSC™ paper
to ensure responsible forest management.

For more information visit: www.harpercollins.co.uk/green

In loving memory of
Philip Travis Rawlinson 1957–2021.

My rock throughout my ordeal and friend to the end.

CONTENTS

PROLOGUE

I can picture precisely where I was when my life imploded. On a warm August afternoon, I received a telephone call from my sister-in-law. I had never had the chance to properly talk with her, but now she was phoning with a warning: 'I hope you're not financially involved with Alexander.'

Those eight words changed everything. Soon I would learn that Alexander de Rothschild, the man who had swept me off my feet nearly four years earlier, and to whom I had given my heart, was nothing but a callous conman. A conman who had taken everything I had.

It was the start of an odyssey of discovery. As I peeled back layer after layer of my new life, I slowly navigated my way to the truth. The person I knew as Alexander de Rothschild was a construct. His web of deceit was so vast and complex that even the police couldn't fully untangle it.

But he reserved his greatest con for me. He took my money, he took my peace of mind – and he changed the shape of my life forever.

This is my story. It is one of betrayal, but also of the strength of the human spirit.

1

A CHILDHOOD

For all the financial loss that came to dominate my later life, my upbringing, like that of so many, was modest.

Mum was born in Tewkesbury and she met Dad while he was doing his national service at Ashchurch Army Camp; he used to visit the milkshake bar where she was working at the time. Not long afterwards, they were married at Tewkesbury Abbey on 26 December 1954. They were both young – eighteen and twenty respectively – but that wasn't unusual back then.

Children came along quickly too: Karen was born first when Mum was nineteen, followed three years later by Diane, then another two years later by Dawn. Mum was twenty-nine when she had me. I suspect I was my parents' last attempt to give Dad the boy he longed for after first one daughter, then another. When I was older, I'd often see him shaking his head in exasperation, muttering, 'I've got a house full of bloody women.'

Six foot tall and very handsome, Dad always wore his hair slicked back in a quiff. Like Mum, who was one of eight, he came from a big family, and they were very important to him; he had one tattoo on his arm that read 'The sweetest girl I ever kissed was another man's wife, my mother'. For the first couple of years of their married life Mum and Dad lived with Dad's parents and his three siblings at their home in Shotton, a small Flintshire town, which borders the River Dee. Karen and Di were born there, but by the time Mum fell pregnant with Dawn, Dad had managed to rent a steelworker's house in the Garden City estate. He'd been a steelworker at the John Summers Steelworks since he was fourteen. Aside from his national service, he would work there his entire life, seeing it morph first into British Steel and then Tata Steel, before retiring at sixty-five.

Both he and Mum lived out their days in the Garden City estate home, the same house I live in today. Now, though, the estate is barely recognisable from the sprawling, friendly working-class neighbourhood where I grew up. Back then everyone's front doors were kept open, and we had a degree of freedom unimaginable to today's kids. There were lots of other children on the estate whose parents worked at the steelworks, and we ran around as a pack. In summer we were out all hours, scrumping apples, playing ball and building dens, coming home dirty and exhausted as dusk fell or when we were hungry – whichever came first.

Our house was modest: a two-up, two-down semi-detached affair with a good-sized back garden and an outside loo. Even today, decades on and having had proper indoor plumbing installed, I can still remember the dread of waking up on a winter's night needing to answer the call of nature, and having to head downstairs and out the back door and dash across the freezing yard.

Being freezing was a general childhood theme, in fact: this was long before the days of central heating and on winter mornings – and not always just winter mornings – it was always perishingly cold until Mum got the coal fire going in the kitchen or living room.

All four of us girls shared a bedroom, which was less cramped than it sounds as the room was reasonably large, with a bunk bed in one alcove, a single bed in another and a double bed against a wall. Besides, by the time I was seven Karen had already left home and, at the tender age of seventeen, was expecting a baby of her own. My sisters and I spent hours up in our room, playing make-believe and skating across the rug that lay on the linoleum floor. Karen was the big sister we used to enjoy winding up, Di was the one I felt the most natural connection with, while Dawn was more complicated – funny and clever, but with a sullen streak. As for me, I was quite shy and withdrawn back then. But we all got on well enough, aside from the usual sibling squabbles.

There was never much in the way of money. While Mum had the odd part-time job, she was largely a stay-at-home mum, meaning we had to live on Dad's modest steelworker wages – or what was left once Dad had handed over the housekeeping money. Dad always provided for the family, but like many men of his ilk, his life revolved around work and going to the pub. Working in a foundry was hot and dirty labour, and the first thing the men wanted to do when their shift ended was head to the local for a cooling pint.

Dad was a big community man too, though. He was chairman of the local branch of the Royal British Legion and organised a lot of functions for people in the area, from coach trips to the coast to big family cinema trips at Christmas.

I loved Dad, but I was closer to Mum, who in her younger days had resembled Ingrid Bergman, although her trim figure turned thick-set with age after having four children. A real home bird, family was everything to her, but she had a wicked sense of humour underneath her placid exterior; there was a lot of laughter in the house, and Mum and Dad knew how to have fun. Thursday evening was their night out at the Legion, and us girls would often hear them coming back a bit tipsy, giggling as they came through the front door.

But, as for most people, family life wasn't all plain sailing. Dad had a temper on him, and my parents often argued over money. After paying the bills and feeding and clothing us all, there was very little left over – although, as Mum often pointed out, there was somehow always enough for those after-work pints.

One memory in particular stands out: when I was about ten, Mum brought home a lamp that she'd seen in a local shop and coveted for weeks. As people often did back then, she'd asked the shopkeeper if she could put a down payment on it, and had given him fifty pence a week until she'd finally paid off the balance. She was thrilled with this lamp, which had a clear round base containing artificial flowers – this was the early Seventies, remember! But not long after she brought it home Dad came home half cut one night and the two of them started arguing about money again. I listened from the top of

the stairs, half fascinated, half appalled. The fight quickly esca-
lated, with Dad shouting, 'You've got money to buy that piece
of crap,' then promptly karate-chopping the lampshade right
off. In return, Mum picked up the base and smashed it over
his head. We woke the next morning to find Dad – with a
sore head that owed as much to an epic hangover as my mum's
decision to use her beloved lamp as a weapon – picking bits of
glass out of the carpet and his head. My sisters and I still talk
about it to this day.

But there was more to my family than manual labour and
working-class dramas: there was an undercurrent of spiritual-
ism too. My maternal grandmother had been a medium who
used to hold seances: Mum once told me she had walked into
the room just in time to see someone's tie lift straight up from
their shirt, as if an invisible hand was pulling it. The sight had
freaked her out, lodging in her memory forever and making
her determined to steer clear of anything supernatural.

My dad was the opposite: as I progressed through my teenage years, he transferred his loyalties from the local church to
a spiritualist church in Chester. He'd always been interested in
life after death, and over time this interest spiralled into other,
more unworldly matters, especially after someone at the
church told him they thought he could be a healer. He started
to explore the idea with others who were interested at the local
church and on occasion used his newfound skills on friends
and family members.

Mum didn't like it when Dad came home with his stories of
miracle recoveries. 'I've seen stuff with my own eyes, Roy –
and I don't want to believe it,' she'd tell him. I wasn't sure

what to make of it either, although I did have an odd experience years later, when I was living in Cheltenham. I had found a spiritual church for Dad to attend when he came to visit, and the medium came over and gave him a long message, punctuated with the names of people I didn't know, but Dad seemed to understand. I can still picture the tears trickling down his face. So I was definitely not a total sceptic.

There is one thing that strikes me in particular when I look back on my childhood: there was little to no ambition in our family home. Mum had never had a lot of choices when she was growing up; like many of her class and era, she'd been raised to believe that a woman's destiny was to raise children. She'd never questioned that, and it was a belief she carried through to her own daughters. She just assumed that, like her, we would get married and have babies by our early twenties.

It was a path that Karen and Dawn took, and I could easily have gone down the same road too. There was certainly very little encouragement at school to do much else. The large local comprehensive my sisters and I attended from the age of eleven was decent enough, but its main mission seemed to be getting the students out the other end without incident. Very few went to university, and beyond the armed forces, the chicken factory, the steelworks or hairdressing, the 'careers officer' – if you can call her that – had very little else in the way of suggestions for our future. It was hard to be inspired, and so while I wasn't an unruly student, I didn't put much effort in. Even so, I was above average in the classroom, and sometimes I wonder how I would have got on if I'd actually knuckled down.

Although I didn't realise it at the time, things changed for me when I was around fourteen and started babysitting for Christine and Steve, who lived down the road from my family. Like Dad, Steve worked shifts at the steelworks, but while they also had four children, Christine, unlike Mum, also held down various jobs. Their double income helped to fund the purchase of a small boat, a VW caravanette and a Land Rover.

Steve and Christine were active types. Most weekends they went diving in the quarries of North Wales, while Easter and summer breaks were spent camping in Anglesey. As I got to know them better they invited me along, and while in theory I was there to help out with the kids, over time I felt more like a member of the family.

I have very fond memories of our holidays together. Steve was a larger-than-life character with a guttural laugh and, together with Christine, he tried to teach me to water-ski and dive. We fished off the boat and I caught pollock and mackerel.

The crowd on Anglesey was different to anything I was used to. The people I met there came from nice postcodes in leafy parts of Cheshire. They were doctors, teachers and engineers who had nicer clothes, bigger cars and broader horizons. Looking back, those weekends sitting on Anglesey's windswept beaches playing with teenagers from more affluent backgrounds – whose borders weren't limited to the Garden City estate – helped expand my vision and my understanding of the wider world.

It wasn't something I picked up on straight away, though. After leaving school at sixteen, I got a youth training scheme job in the local post office. I loved it, but it only lasted six months and once the government had stopped paying my wages there was no job for me to go on to. I was at a loose end, until one of the girls I'd befriended on Anglesey got in touch. A family friend who ran a restaurant was looking for waiting staff at his place in Chester. It wasn't exactly a big step up on the career ladder, but coming from Garden City, the sophisticated medieval centre of Chester felt as metropolitan as New York. It was only six miles away from my parents' house, but it might as well have been another planet.

At first I travelled to and from my shifts, but often after working late I'd stay over with my friend. Over time I went home less and less. Mum and Dad didn't mind – they were used to me coming and going, and I'm sure that after nearly thirty years of child-rearing Mum was looking forward to getting the last one off her hands. So when Jan, a friend who lived on the other side of Chester, suggested we pool our resources and get our own place nearer to the centre I jumped at the chance. Jan had split up with her boyfriend and I had just come out of a relationship, so the timing felt right. Shortly before my eighteenth birthday I left home for good, deter-mined to be independent.

I could never have imagined that forty years later I would be back.

2

BECOMING MRS HANDY

'Three burgers and two milkshakes for table three, chef.' I slapped the order on the counter and wondered if I might have time to nip out for a cheeky cigarette. On a busy Friday it was hard to get even a minute to yourself.

The burger bar, which was called Sixties American Restaurant, was in competition with another chain called the Great American Disaster, both of them exploiting the Sixties nostalgia that was already in full swing in the early Eighties. The décor was deliberately retro, all low-slung ceiling lights and televisions fixed to the wall playing music videos, mostly the Beach Boys. While it wasn't exactly a dream job, I enjoyed working there – the team were a good bunch and most of the time the customers were nice too.

Jan had a job in Chester as well, in a menswear shop. But not long after we moved in together the shop burned down and she was relocated to their Manchester branch. One night, she came home and asked if I wanted a change of scene.

'There's a jewellery concession in the shop that they need someone to run,' she said. 'Why don't you apply? If you get the job, we can travel in and out together.' I didn't have anything to lose; it wasn't as if my job at the burger bar was taking me anywhere. So I applied and promptly got the job.

It was the cue for a particularly happy, carefree period. I was nineteen, living away from home with no responsibilities other than to earn enough to pay my rent and bills. The rest was for fun, and Jan and I certainly had plenty of that. We'd have to leave our little one-bedroom flat in the centre of Chester at 6 a.m. to get into Manchester in time for work, and we often wouldn't get home till 6 o'clock at night, but then, after something to eat and sometimes a little catnap, we'd go out clubbing until the small hours. We were burning the candle at both ends, but if you can't do that when you're nineteen then when can you?

We were often joined at the weekends by my Uncle Tim, Mum's younger brother. Only ten years older than me, he was more like a brother, and we'd always got on well. Once I'd got my own flat Tim would often drive up on Saturday morning from his two-bedroom cottage on the outskirts of a farm in Tewkesbury and we'd take him clubbing. In turn, Jan and I would jump on a coach to go and stay with him, spending riotous nights out at the Plough in Elmley Castle, a tiny pub with a big reputation. The pub itself was small, but the real action took place in the car park where every weekend an eclectic mix of hippies, bikers and the town's bohemian crowd would gather to down the fifty-pence pints of cider.

One early summer weekend in 1985, Tim was staying with us when Jan and I got a call from our manager saying that now the Manchester store had burned down, leaving us both without a job. Although we had enough to pay the coming month's rent, I wasn't convinced we'd find another job in time to fund the following month's outgoings. Jokingly I said to Jan that I might have to go cap in hand to the burger bar and get my old waitressing shifts back. Tim was having none of it. 'Look,' he said, 'you don't have any ties here. I've got space at my place. Why don't you chuck your stuff in the back of the car and come and live in Tewkesbury?'

It was as good an idea as any. We spent the rest of the day frenziedly hurling our shoes and clothes into big bags and into the boot of Uncle Tim's old Mercedes before driving to Tewkesbury – together with his newly purchased tarantula, Chester, in a box under the passenger seat. It was the start of another new chapter.

Somewhere in Uncle Tim's possession is a photo album called 'The Summer of 1985', and it records a blur of drinking, dancing and parties. We had a wild old time of it that summer. There were nights out at pubs, gigs and house parties, before everyone would pile back to Tim's cottage. It was surrounded by fields and farmland so there was plenty of space, and at times it felt like we were holding our own mini festival.

Those nights out had to be funded somehow, though, so Jan and I both got jobs on a factory production line sorting frozen fruit at Tewkesbury Cold Store. It wasn't exactly inspiring work, but it allowed me to pay my way, and three months in the manager came over and asked me if I'd like to apply for a receptionist's job. They obviously really wanted me to do it because despite me having nothing in the way of experience they gave me the job.

Around this time I met a girl called Clare at one of Uncle Tim's many parties. Tall and slim with blue eyes and a mop of unruly blonde hair, Clare was privately educated, bright, funny and very confident. Her family had a successful business, which meant that background-wise we were chalk and cheese, but we hit it off, and often met up at lunchtimes or for a drink after work.

Uncle Tim had started to drop hints that it was time for us to get a place of our own, so Jan got new lodgings with one of Uncle Tim's friends, and I moved into a caravan with another friend of his. Not long afterwards, Clare split up with her boyfriend and asked if I wanted to share the rent on a house in Cheltenham, which was owned by the water board where she worked. It was perfect timing (for me, at least) so I took her up on it straight away.

Clare and I worked hard and played hard. But Clare also had her sights set higher. One evening, as we flopped on the sofa with a glass of wine, she announced that she wanted to do a round-the-world trip.

'Come with me, Chrissy,' she pleaded.

I couldn't think of anything I would rather do more – but there was no way I could afford the £1,000 cost of the ticket. Undeterred, Clare – who was nothing if not determined – said she would pay for my ticket and that when we returned I could set up a Direct Debit and pay her back monthly. She suggested that in the meantime I take on extra work and save for my living expenses.

We went to the local travel agent as soon as we could. I felt the bubbles of excitement in my stomach as we started to tick off the destinations we would hit. Los Angeles. Sydney. Auckland. They were all a very long way from Garden City.

The plan was to leave in October 1987 for a trip lasting roughly six months – which left me a year to get some money in the bank. Alongside my work at the Cold Stores, I got a bar job in a local pub called the Restoration, and weekend shifts at an estate agent. I was permanently knackered, but I knew it would be worth it. On winter mornings, when I was scrambling to get out of bed to do another shift and all I wanted to do was snuggle back under the duvet, I reminded myself that at some point in the not-too-distant future I would be drinking in the freedom of open roads and wide blue skies.

The only blot on the landscape was that, shortly after planning our trip, both Clare and I acquired boyfriends. She had taken up with an old flame from school while I had got together with Paul, a chartered surveyor and a regular at the Restoration, where he would stand at the end of the bar with his drinking buddies. After moving out of the place I shared with Clare, I lived on my own for a few months before shacking up with Paul. Although the relationship was pretty serious and from the outset Paul was supportive of my wanderlust, I still thought he might end things as the day of my departure approached – this was long before the days when social media and mobile phones made it easy to keep in regular touch. To my surprise he was insistent that he would wait for me. 'Just go and have a good time, Chrissy,' he said. 'I'll still be here when you get back.'

* * *

Our trip was everything I'd hoped for and more, an unfurling dream of sun-drenched days filled with adventure and new experiences. We kicked off by spending a few days in LA, staying in the Hollywood Hills with a university friend of Clare's, then hired a car and drove along the great Pacific Coast Highway to San Francisco. From there we went to New Zealand and travelled round the North and South islands. Our next stop was Sydney where we explored the city for a week before flying to Cairns, hiring a car and driving down the coast all the way to Adelaide via Sydney again and Melbourne. We came home via two weeks in Bali, a week in Bangkok and a last-minute diversion to Dusseldorf to stay with some German friends we'd met on the road.

We flew back into Heathrow on a sunny March morning, and despite the blue skies and the hint of spring in the air, I promptly burst into tears. It had all been so magical that I simply didn't want it to end. I felt like going into the cockpit, grabbing the controls of the plane and taking it somewhere – anywhere – else. I just wanted to keep going.

Paul knew that I would be feeling a bit flat, so in order to try to counterbalance my return to normality he'd booked a fishing trip to Northern Ireland. 'You don't have to face reality yet,' he told me as we drove to Belfast. I was so grateful, but there was no escaping the fact that my lengthy trip away had unsettled me. I didn't know what I wanted from life any more – and that included Paul. A few weeks after I got home, we split up, and I moved out of Paul's house into a small basement flat in Cheltenham owned by Clare's brother.

By then I'd also got another new job. A friend of Paul's who owned a coffee shop and delicatessen called the Shambles in the centre of Cheltenham offered me a job there, which I started in March 1988.

The Shambles was a lively, busy place, and well known in the town. Decked out with church pews and old sewing-machine tables, it also had a lovely courtyard seating area. I worked there nine hours a day, five days a week, and like any waitress worth her salt I quickly got to know several of the regular customers.

Among them was Clive Handy. Eleven years older than me and very handsome, Clive was seen as an incredibly eligible Cotswold bachelor whose parents owned Hampton Manor, a 250-year-old Cotswold farmhouse set amid 400 acres of land, which they farmed.

I didn't chat to Clive much at first. While he would often catch my eye and smile, I thought he would be a great match for Clare, who was also single again. The two of them had the same kind of affluent background and easy confidence. But to my amazement it wasn't Clare he was interested in. One evening, Karen, the daughter of the café owner, who had become a good friend, invited a gang of us round to her flat for dinner. Clive was there, and as the riotous evening of eating and drinking games unfolded I was struck by what easy company he was. When, a couple of days later, he asked me out for a drink it seemed entirely natural to say yes.

Nothing romantic happened on that first night, which we spent in a local pub playing bar billiards and chatting about our backgrounds. Clive was easy to talk to, and although I was keenly aware that we came from very different worlds, it didn't seem to make any difference – at least not until Clive invited me and Karen to the family farm for a walk. As Karen's car arrived at the top of the lane leading to his family home, I could hardly believe my eyes. Below me, at the end of a chestnut-tree-lined drive, lay a stunning honey-coloured farmhouse, surrounded by outbuildings and land. For some- one from a housing estate in the North-west it seemed like Downton Abbey, and my instinct was to get Karen to turn the car around. I felt daunted.

Of course, Karen was having none of it. 'Don't be ridicu- lous, Chrissy,' she said. 'You know Clive well enough by now. And besides, I think he's quite keen on you.'

We went for a lovely walk through the Cotswolds country- side, and when Karen said she had to leave to meet someone, Clive suggested I stay and offered to run me home later. To my surprise I found myself saying yes without hesitation.

That night, Clive took me for supper in the local pub and, on the way back, pausing under a canopy of trees, we shared our first kiss. It's odd, but deep down, right then and there, I knew this man was my future husband. It wasn't a rush of heady romantic excitement, but it was the first time I had ever felt this sense of conviction.

Nonetheless, Clive's life took some adjusting to. His was a world of wingback chairs, of set mealtimes, shooting parties and hunt balls. As our romance unfolded I often felt like a fish out of water and would periodically be gripped by self-doubt, amazed that he was interested in this working-class girl. While Clive's parents, Robert and Joan, were welcoming, I couldn't shake the feeling that deep down they too felt that their beloved eldest son would be better off marrying a local well-to-do country girl – and that I should be grateful that he had chosen me instead.

The months unfolded and around a year after we'd met I left my job in Cheltenham – by then I'd moved on from the Shambles – and took on another role as an assistant house manager at Salperton Park, a large local country house, which held conferences, weddings and shooting parties. I enjoyed the new challenge, and Clive was thrilled that I was embracing country life. Yet by now we were unfortunately starting to have some fights. After a particularly upsetting one at a wedding of friend of Clive's in a village called Brockhampton, I thought, 'Screw this.' I didn't have a car, but I wasn't going to let that – or the fact that it was pitch black and I was wearing high-heeled shoes – stop me. Without a backward glance I left the wedding and started to embark on the twelve-mile walk home to Cheltenham. About five miles into the walk, on a remote road with no footpath, a passing police car pulled over and an officer asked me what on earth I was doing.

'Jump in and we'll take you back to the party,' one officer said, after I'd explained why I was there. I said no, unless they wanted a murder on their hands, at which point they laughed and offered to run me back into town. Clive turned up in the small hours, full of apologies, and we made up.

We may have argued from time to time, but we were generally happy, and when, in September 1990, two years after we'd first met, Clive proposed on a camping trip at Corfe Castle as we nestled in our tent following a meal at a local pub, I accepted without hesitation. Love is a powerful distraction.

I was twenty-seven and Clive was thirty-eight when we married on 16 February 1991 at Salperton church, followed by a reception at Salperton Park. I loved my dress – a long-sleeved ivory silk number made for me by a friend who had taken the trouble to embroider our initials on the train like a Chanel logo – and Clive looked exceptionally handsome in his morning suit.

It was a happy day, notwithstanding my anxieties about my family, who were arriving mob-handed on a minibus and who I knew would be every bit as overwhelmed as I was at first by this unfamiliar environment. I was very aware of helping them feel relaxed and comfortable, so while I had to do the rounds of Clive's family and friends, I made sure I spent as much time as I could with them. In the end they enjoyed themselves, although my sisters have since told me that they couldn't believe their eyes at the new world their little sister had found herself in as they rattled down Cotswolds country lanes.

By then, of course, I was getting used to it all. Life felt good and full of promise – although, as I was soon to find out, the honeymoon period was not going to last long.

3

AN ENDING AND A BEGINNING

The wedding gifts had barely been packed away before my relationship doubts turned into the first signs of marital cracks. Clive was fundamentally a good man, but like everyone he sometimes struggled with his emotions. He was determined for us to live a traditional life, which I found suffocating at times. Of course, this didn't all happen overnight, and after returning from honeymoon in Kenya we were both plunged headlong into farm – and family – life.

By way of a wedding present, Clive's parents had given us half of their old manor house, and during our fortnight away the builders had been blocking up old doorways, installing new wiring and plumbing and putting in stone mullion windows. We were also having a new kitchen built in the oldest part of the building, which had once been a cattle shed.

I still had my job managing events at Salperton Park, but I had my farm duties too, which involved everything from helping with the harvest to shearing sheep. I even learned how to reverse a tractor and trailer, and would follow the combine harvester, unloading grain into my trailer. I actually really

enjoyed the farm work, although I resented Clive's dad boss-
ing me around like a farmhand – something I frequently
complained to Clive about. Sometimes it felt like his dad
could literally sniff when I had a moment to myself. Whenever
I did, he would appear at the kitchen door saying he could use
me outside.

He also treated our half of the manor house as if he still
lived in it. I lost count of the mornings when I would be in
my dressing gown having a cup of tea when Robert would
walk straight in through the kitchen door. It felt like an intru-
sion, particularly for someone like me who had previously
been so independent. It was clear I hadn't just married just
Clive; I had married his family.

I'll be honest: there were quite a few days during the first
year of my marriage when I could have cried. It all felt a bit
too much. As far as I was concerned, though, I was stuck with
it. I wasn't naive or romantic, but I did think you married for
life. Mum and Dad's relationship was no picnic, but they were
married for sixty years. I never thought for one minute that
my own marriage would come to an end.

Of course, there were fun times too. We had a good crowd
of friends, and every Thursday we'd go to the local pub for a
steak and a pint. There were trips to London, nice holidays
and visits to see my family, who were very fond of Clive.
Nonetheless, there was no getting away from the fact that my
independent days were long behind me. Not long after we'd
got married Clive suggested I give up my job at Salperton,
due to the late nights involved. The decision meant that I
went from clearing £2,000 a month take-home pay – a decent

amount of money even now, and definitely back then – to £80 a week for helping out on the farm. As I used to joke (and later complain) to Clive, it was barely enough to cover the price of a pair of wellies.

Walking away from Salperton meant that I didn't really have anything that was just mine and it niggled away at me, together with the fact that I'd never completed any formal education. Around two years into the marriage, I decided to take night classes to train as a beautician. It took me out of the house for three hours twice a week, and while Clive wasn't thrilled about it, he couldn't exactly stop it. Plus, it gave us some welcome extra income. Against the backdrop of my dramatic salary cut, any additional money I could bring in waxing bikini lines and painting nails would come in handy.

It was during the course, in late 1993, that we found out I was pregnant with Tom. I was thrilled, as was Clive. We hadn't rushed into parenthood immediately, but after a couple of years of marriage both of us felt ready. Tom – or the seventh Thomas Handy of Hampen, to give him his full title – was born in June 1994 and from the moment he was put into my arms I was in love. Tom had colic so he wasn't the easiest baby, but even with all the sleepless nights I loved everything about becoming a mum. I still do. Even now my kids laugh at me and call me a Mother Hen. I was a practical, hands-on sort of mum and didn't let stuff get me down. Like any new mum, I had moments when I felt a bit bewildered and overwhelmed, but I used to just pop Tom in a papoose and carry him around with me as I did my housework and jobs on the farm.

It wasn't long before I got pregnant again, only for my pregnancy to end in miscarriage. It was traumatic, but I got pregnant again fairly quickly and my second son Simon was born in August 1996.

I went into hospital on the evening of 24 August and gave birth at 6 a.m. the following day with Clive by my side. Six hours later I was discharged, but I had barely climbed out of the passenger side of the car with my hours-old newborn son before Clive said he needed a favour. Apparently the combine harvester had hit a badger sett and been damaged in the process, and it needed a new part.

'Chrissy, we're really stuck,' Clive told me. 'There's no way any of us here can spare the time to get away as I need to get back to see if I can get it up and running again. Is there any chance you could drive to Andoversford and pick it up?'

The correct answer to that question was of course 'no', but like the dutiful wife I was I turned round, popped Simon back into his car seat and drove into Andoversford, where there was a large agricultural machinery depot called TH White.

I arrived at TH White in the early afternoon only to bump into one of Clive's friends who had happened to come in at the same time. 'What on *earth* are you doing here?' he asked. 'You've just given birth!'

I was asking myself the same question. In fact, it was starting to dawn on me that while on paper I was Clive's wife, much of the time I felt like a farmhand, earning my keep. Certainly, the other wives I knew didn't do half as much as I did. They always seemed to be meeting friends for lunch or going shopping. Meanwhile, I was juggling helping out on the farm with raising the kids and, in time, running a part-time beautician's outfit from a room I had converted at home.

As the months went on relations between Clive and me were deteriorating, but to my surprise he was still keen for us to have another baby.

'Come on, Chrissy, it'd be nice to have three, wouldn't it?' he said.

The odd thing was that I agreed with him. I adored being a mum and while it had become clear to me that I didn't have the best marriage, it didn't mean we couldn't still have a lovely family.

Sarah was born in March 1999, a gorgeous petite little thing with a mop of fine blonde hair. It was another immediate love affair.

Nonetheless, any mum of three will know what those early years are like. There was barely a moment to catch my breath, let alone think about the future. But there was no getting away from the fact that our relationship was strained. Clive wasn't a bad person; he loved the kids very much and most of the time he was a great dad. But it didn't make up for the fact that I was becoming increasingly miserable. I felt trapped. I'd been raised to understand that life wasn't easy, and that you were always going to go through difficult patches, but I'd started to feel unloved. Sometimes I would wake up feeling pretty hopeless about the future.

As it was, things came to a head in the summer of 2002. Our neighbour, Annie, ran an events management company, and from time to time when she was short-staffed she would ask me to help her out. It was well paid, and although it was hard work, it was fun too – I had a few days in Barcelona and on another occasion was flown out to Tenerife. In spring that year, Annie asked if I could help her out at an event on Lake Garda. It would be long hours, but it meant some independence, and while Clive wasn't thrilled about being home alone with the kids, he knew the money was good. Besides, I'd already made up my mind. I was very unhappy and needed some time away. In late June I flew into Milan, and from there was driven to a beautiful hotel not far from the lake, where I was going to work front of house, ensuring the delegates attending the conference had everything they needed.

I worked alongside the hotel manager – a rather handsome Italian man called Luka. We got to know each other well over those ten days, working what felt like round the clock. The hotel was in the grounds of a very large farm, so we often talked about farming. On the last day of the conference, he gave me a guided tour around the estate, then on into the local village where he introduced me to some of his friends over a bottle of wine. Perhaps it was inevitable, but before I knew it I was back at Luka's place. Even as we undressed, I knew a line had been crossed: it wasn't just that I was cheating on my husband, but the tenderness that Luka showed me exposed the gaping emotional hole at the centre of my life. I knew this romance was nothing more than a one-night stand, but I also knew it was a seismic shift in my sensibilities. I wasn't proud of myself for cheating, but I had only done it because I was incredibly unhappy. It made me realise what I was missing in my relationship.

Even so, I vowed to try to make things work with Clive for the sake of the children – although it was getting harder and harder to paper over the cracks. In July 2002, after a holiday in Brittany marked by escalating and furious rows, it was dawning on me that this wasn't going to get any better. I had sleepless nights trying to work out what to do. I still felt that you mated for life, no matter what, and pulling that apart felt overwhelming – not just practically, but emotionally. At the same time, I knew I couldn't go on like this.

In the event, everything came to a head on the night of 23 August. Clive and I had had another row over something and nothing once the kids had gone to bed, which had ended with him leaving the house and getting into his car. Listening to the screech of the wheels on the drive as he roared away was a sobering moment. Almost on autopilot, I went upstairs, got the kids out of bed, put them in the back of my people carrier, grabbed my handbag, shut the door behind me and left. It was 10 p.m., and our marriage of eleven years was over.

It was only as I turned down the driveway into the country lane that I realised I didn't know where I was going. It was too late to turn up on my parents' doorstep, so instead I pitched up at my sister Diane's. I'd left so hastily that the first thing I had to do after settling the kids in was drive to the nearest twenty-four-hour supermarket to get them each something to wear, a toothbrush and toothpaste.

Devastated to arrive home to an empty house, Clive rang my parents, then eventually tracked me down to Di's, where he tried everything to get the marriage back on track. I told him it was too late now – we'd just end up rehashing the same old arguments. It meant that I was always going to be cast as the bad guy, but that seemed to be a small price to pay for freedom and a fresh start.

Obviously, I couldn't stay at Di's for ever, and after a few days I returned to Cheltenham, initially to stay with friends, and then to rent a property in nearby Bishops Cleeve. Those early months weren't easy – no matter how much you yearn to be free of a marriage you still mourn the ending of it, not just for the hopes you once had but for your children, of whom you have robbed the chance to live under the same roof as their mum and dad until they are old enough to create a home of their own. The road to divorce is always rocky too, dotted with rows, particularly when the thorny issue of money rears its head. Even so, in time Clive and I were able to build an amicable enough relationship.

Our divorce was finalised in October 2003, when I was thirty-nine. As part of the settlement, I got a lump sum of £650,000. I was able to buy myself a decent home in the form of a lovely three-storey, red-brick Victorian house on All Saints Road in a leafy suburb of Cheltenham. It had five bedrooms, three bathrooms, two reception rooms and a huge kitchen, and while it was spacious it was also homely. I was excited about what I saw as a fresh start for me and the kids following months of upheaval.

However the combination of maintenance payments and tax credits left me £800 a month to live on, which wasn't enough to cover outgoings without drawing down on the limited amount of money left over from the settlement once

I'd bought my house. So, I started a business course at Gloucestershire University to enhance my employment opportunities and took a part-time job in a clothing boutique called Feva. The income, small as it was, was a handy supplement to my life as a newly single woman, and it meant I didn't have to dip into the money left over from my lump-sum payment once I'd bought my new family home. It had been a big leap of faith to leave Clive, but it seemed like everything was working out – for now.

4

A MAN CALLED ALEXANDER

'Do you mind if I take this seat?' A simple question that would change my life – not that I knew it back then, on that otherwise nondescript June morning in 2003.

The day had started much like any other. Just as I had been doing for several weeks, I'd popped into a coffee shop in Cheltenham called Soho in-between dropping my children off at school and starting my shift at Feva at 10 a.m. I settled down happily at an outside table – my preference as a smoker – with my coffee and a copy of the *Daily Telegraph*. I had only been there for five minutes or so when a polite, well-spoken voice asked if he could sit down.

'Help yourself,' I said, barely glancing up. I was engrossed in the newspaper spread in front of me, and just assumed that the rest of the tables were taken. So when I looked up again five minutes later, I was surprised to realise that the entire seating area was empty save for the new arrival at my own table: a well-dressed man in a suit who was notably more smartly attired than the average passer-by in the area. Perhaps he saw the flicker of puzzlement that flashed across my face, because at that point my unexpected table companion struck up a conversation.

'Anything interesting?' he asked, gesturing to the newspaper in front of me. I'll be honest: I didn't want a chat. Not with him, not with anyone. My divorce was still ongoing and it was painful and draining, involving an endless litany of solicitors' letters and sometimes angry and emotional conversations. My main focus was trying to keep things as calm as possible for the children, and there were days when I felt like I was constantly treading on eggshells. My morning coffee before work was one of the few occasions during the week when I wasn't either embroiled in the domestic duties of motherhood or dealing with the ongoing fallout from my separation with Clive.

All I wanted to do was bury my head in the paper again. But I'd been raised not to be rude and so with the best half-smile I could muster – one that I hoped seemed pleasant enough but would send a reasonably robust signal that I wasn't really in the mood for talking – I said something about it all seeming to be bad news these days. It was all he needed.

'Well, I thought *you* looked interesting,' he smiled.

I was a bit taken aback. While it wasn't entirely unheard of for me to be chatted up – back then, I was a slim size 12 and, courtesy of my job, I had to take care of myself and dress smartly – I had no interest at all in being asked out on a date. I had enough going on.

Undeterred, my table companion carried on, telling me that he came into Cheltenham every Monday morning to do his banking. He had, he told me, spotted me in the coffee shop a couple of times before. There was no getting away from a conversation now, so with an inward sigh I folded my newspaper and asked him whether he lived locally. He had been here just a few months, he replied, after a long period abroad courtesy of his work as a consultant. I asked if he worked at the local hospital and, laughing, he told me he wasn't a medical consultant but a financial one.

'I'm Alexander,' he said, putting out his hand.

'Chrissy,' I said, offering mine.

We chatted for the next ten minutes until, glancing at my watch, I realised I had to go. Although my shift at Feva didn't start for another half an hour, I needed to buy a birthday card for someone as there would be no time between work ending and picking up the kids from school.

'Nice to meet you,' I said, as I gathered up my handbag and coat and started to make my way down the street. I honestly thought I would never see him again.

In fact, I saw Alexander again a week later when I returned to the coffee shop. This time, I walked in to find him ahead of me, already buying his cappuccino.

'Hi, Chrissy,' he said brightly, apparently surprised. 'You're here again.'

Whether he had waited for me I will never know, but in the moment it didn't cross my mind that it was anything other than a coincidence, particularly as he had told me that he came to Cheltenham every week, so it seemed natural enough to take a seat together. Conversation flowed easily: general chit-chat about life and my kids, who were my main focus at that time apart from my divorce – and I certainly wasn't going to talk to a stranger about that. Alexander, meanwhile, was happy to talk about himself a lot, and in particular his work. He went on at some length about the fact that he was studying alongside his consultancy work as he wanted to go back to university to do a business course with the aim of becoming a professor in mathematical modelling.

'How on earth are you going to hold down a job and study at the same time?' I asked.

'Most professors are part-time,' he replied. 'A lot of them are doing both.'

As it did on the first occasion, this time our encounter ended with little more than casual pleasantries. 'Nice to see you again,' I said, as I gathered up my newspaper and handbag. 'Maybe see you around.'

I meant it as little more than a sign-off – but the following Monday when I arrived at the coffee shop Alexander was already there, and this time there was a coffee waiting for me at his table. I thought it was a bit presumptuous, although I was also rather touched. In a world where it sometimes felt like I was running around like a whirling dervish trying to sort out everybody else's problems, it was nice that someone had thought to do something for me, however small. This time the conversation had a more intimate, familiar feel too. Alexander told me more about his family. His full name was Alexander d'Ariken; his mother, Philomena, was Chinese, and he had been born in Singapore, the eldest of four siblings. He had two sisters called Lydia and Theresa who were both barristers and a brother, Mason, who was a company director. His father Peter had sadly died when he was seven.

Back then, of course, they were nothing more than names being shared across a coffee table. He also told me about his life so far, which had come a long way from those early days. He was so bright that he'd got a scholarship first to Westminster, then Eton, where he proved such an outstanding pupil that he had got into Oxford University at fifteen years old. He had a degree as an engineer and also as an economist. It was certainly an impressive CV, and one I didn't question. Why would I? One of my sisters always liked to tell me that I tend to believe the best in people. 'You're a bit naive sometimes, Chrissy,' she'd said more than once.

It was at the end of that third meeting, as I finished my coffee and prepared to head over to Feva, that Alexander asked me for my number. 'I'd like to take you out for dinner, Chrissy,' he said, gazing at me earnestly across the table.

I'll admit I was flattered. It had been a long time since anyone had asked me on a date, and it's a rare woman who doesn't like a confidence boost. Nonetheless, my resolve was firm. 'That's a lovely offer, Alexander, but I'm not looking to date anyone,' I told him. 'So it's a no to my number. I hope you understand.'

'Oh,' he said, looking crestfallen. 'That's a shame. Would you mind if I gave you my number, then maybe if you changed your mind you could drop me a line?' He looked so wounded that, soft touch that I am, I found myself relenting almost immediately.

'Look, you can have my number,' I said, shaking my head with a smile at how quickly he had won me over. 'I won't do dinner but perhaps we can go out for lunch.'

'That would be lovely,' he said. 'I'll drop you a text.'

Looking back, it's amazing how quickly it all happened. Nor did he waste his time before following up – in fact, it was a matter of seconds. Moments after I walked through the door of Feva to start my shift my phone pinged with a message.

'It's been lovely meeting you, Chrissy,' it read. 'You're a really nice lady.'

It was the start of Alex's wooing campaign, which started to gather pace from there. Three days after that first message – one he followed up with a couple more casual messages asking how I was – he walked into Feva during my Thursday-morning shift, knowing he would find me there as I had told him about my part-time job. My boss and I were stocktaking, so I was head down in paperwork and scrutinising the rails of clothes, and I gave a start when I heard my name being called.

'Hi, Chrissy,' the voice said. 'I just called in to see how you were.'

I turned round and there was Alexander, standing in the door sporting a wide grin. I was one part touched, nine parts embarrassed. I'm quite a private person, and while my boss knew I was going through a divorce, we didn't talk about our personal lives particularly. The fact that an unknown man was paying me a call, and one that could be construed as having some kind of romantic undertone, made me feel immensely awkward. I stammered something about it being a busy time and thankfully Alexander seemed to take the hint.

Perhaps I shouldn't have been surprised when he sent me a text message almost immediately afterwards. 'If I can't chat to you at work then we had better make a date for that lunch,' he wrote.

I couldn't help but smile. He was certainly persistent, and there didn't seem to be much harm in meeting for an hour or so.

'How about next Tuesday?' I texted back.

There it was. A date in the diary. Although resolutely NOT, I told myself, a romantic one. Just a chat. I'd had a brief relationship with an old flame shortly after separating from Clive, but when that ended I had resolved to stay single for the foreseeable future.

When I arrived for my lunch date at a local café – my suggestion, as I didn't want anywhere too fancy – I found Alexander waiting for me, clutching a bunch of flowers. It was clear he had shifted his efforts up a gear, although I tried not to think too much about his intentions.

My life was busy, but Alexander seemed determined to find a place in it. Following our lunch, which had unfolded pleasantly enough, he upped his romantic game again. He texted me several times a day, telling me he was falling for me, or sending me song lyrics. One was The Real Thing's 'You to me are everything, the sweetest song that I could sing'; another was 'If you're not the one, then why does my soul feel glad today?' by Daniel Bedingfield. It was cheesy, but rather lovely. It had been years since someone had paid me this much attention, and while my head was telling me not to get involved, my heart was increasingly struggling to listen. On one occasion, over lunch with a good friend, my phone buzzed with another message from him telling me he couldn't stop thinking about me.

'Who's that?' my friend asked, noting that I was smiling as I read it.

'It's that man I mentioned to you, that I met in the coffee shop. He keeps sending me lyrics and lovely messages,' I replied.

'Well, he's certainly keen,' she said. 'Don't knock it!'

It was definitely flattering, but more importantly, I was starting to feel a growing connection with this man who, just over two weeks ago, had been a total stranger. It was exciting to me to have someone whose thoughts and feelings matched mine. When I mentioned I wanted to undertake some charity work he would tell me that he hoped, in time, to set up his own charitable foundation. When I talked about my yearning for a peaceful family life, he would tell me that after his childhood experiences it was all he had ever yearned for too. Whatever my tastes – be it music, food or books – it seemed Alexander's matched. It helped build a growing sense of rapport: here was a man who shared not only my hopes for the future, but my values too. So when, shortly after lunch, he asked if I would now let him take me out to dinner, I agreed. Again, I told myself it didn't *really* mean anything, and that there was no harm in letting someone make me feel good during this stressful time. But three days later the fluttering in my tummy as I pulled on my black top to get ready for our date told a different story. It was the fluttering of excitement and apprehension that I recognised as the early stirrings of someone who was falling in love – whether I liked it or not.

* * *

The place was called the Epicurean, a basement restaurant in a Regency building on Cheltenham's Promenade. It wasn't enormously fancy – more bistro than *haute cuisine* – but it had flattering low lighting and the food was excellent.

We'd arranged to meet at the restaurant, so once my neighbour had arrived to babysit the kids I drove myself there, partly as an insurance policy to ensure I didn't drink too much. Alexander was waiting for me when I got there, tucked away at a corner table and dressed – as he always was in those early days – in a smart suit. He kissed me on the cheek by way of greeting before we sat down and ordered. I was nervous and babbling a bit, cracking jokes in order to keep things light.

Alexander, meanwhile, seemed to be permanently trying to pull the conversation into deeper territory. As we tucked into our main course, he talked about his upbringing in Singapore. After his father Peter had died when he was seven, his mother had remarried a soldier, Fred Hatton, who was then stationed in Singapore. The newly made family were then 'dragged off', as he put it, to Germany, and Alexander had come from there to the UK as a teenager. He didn't like Fred, and his early teenage years were particularly unhappy as he'd been bullied at school, although he didn't tell me why and as it seemed a sensitive area I didn't probe any further.

As pudding arrived, Alexander, staring earnestly at me across the table, said there was something important he needed to tell me. I watched in puzzlement as he reached for his pocket, pulled out his passport and, opening it to the ID page, pushed it across the table.

'I want you to know who I really am, Chrissy,' he said.

I looked down to see the name Alexander Marc Alphonsus Nathaniel d'Ariken de Rothschild-Hatton on the page in front of me alongside his passport photograph. A long name which didn't, in that moment, make much sense to me.

'Gosh, that's a mouthful,' I joked. It was hard to know what to say. Why was he showing me this?

'I'm not sure if you have heard of the Rothschild family,' Alexander said. 'Well, I am one of them. And when I explain it will help you understand some things about me.'

Of course I'd heard of the Rothschild family. Growing up in England in the Sixties, their name was a kind of byword for fabulous wealth. 'Who do you think you are, a Rothschild?' people would joke if they thought you were throwing your money around. Nonetheless it was all so odd that, as was my default, I couldn't help but crack a joke to try to lighten the mood, which had become very intense.

'I've never smoked that brand,' I quipped, referring to the cigarette manufacturer Rothmans.

He didn't smile. 'Chrissy,' he said, reaching for my hand. 'It's really important to me that you know the truth about my background.'

From there it all came out. Alexander told me his real father was Edmond de Rothschild, a pillar of the Rothschild clan and a friend of Peter Ariken (Alexander added the d' later for effect) – the man he now told me had 'adopted' him. Alexander's story was that Edmond de Rothschild had a mistress called Christina Ong – Philomena's best friend at the time. She had died in childbirth, but even before then, when it emerged she had fallen pregnant, Peter had agreed that he and Philomena – who then had no children of their own – would take on the baby and raise it as their own to avoid bringing shame on Edmond's dynasty. Peter and Philomena would go on to have two children of their own: Lydia and Mason, and Philomena would then gone on to have another daughter, Theresa, after marrying Fred.

'Everyone thinks we are blood brothers and sisters, but in fact I am not related to them at all,' he says. 'By rights, I am part heir to the Rothschild fortune. But they will never acknowledge me as one of their own.'

It didn't occur to me to question what he said. Why would I? Alexander had been nothing but warm and sincere, and there hadn't been a single warning bell. In fact, I felt sorry for him. By anyone's standards he'd had a fractured upbringing, losing his 'adoptive' father at seven, then gaining a stepfather who he not only didn't like but who had taken him halfway across the world to two different countries before he'd turned sixteen. He had tried so hard, he said, to get the man he claimed to be his biological father to acknowledge him, but it had always ended in failure.

My head was spinning as, after paying the bill, we walked out of the restaurant towards my car. It was such a lot to take in. I was standing by my car when Alexander leaned forward, put his hand on my cheek and drew my face into his before giving me a lingering, tender kiss, one that I felt in every bone in my body. Despite myself, I went weak at the knees, and it was no longer possible to deny the fact that I was falling for him. I couldn't stop smiling to myself as I drove home, while Alexander, ever the gentleman, telephoned me the moment I got back to tell me what a wonderful evening he'd had, how wonderful I was and how he couldn't wait to see me again.

'I'm falling in love with you, Chrissy,' he said.

'Me too,' I told him. And I meant it.

It would be another week before I could see Alexander again. Our first real date had come in the middle of a particularly busy time, just as I was buying my new home. With my completion date three weeks away and my rental term up in Bishops Cleeve, I had planned to spend the gap first at my mum's house in Flintshire and then in a holiday let at the South Cerney Water Park.

In between the two I had also booked two nights at a hotel in Cheltenham – Alexander's suggestion, as Clive would be taking the children that weekend.

I was at my mum's house for a week. It was the school holidays and I had to keep the children occupied, but Alexander called me constantly. In the evening we would spend hours on the phone. He told me repeatedly he couldn't stop thinking about me, or our kiss.

I arrived at the Cheltenham Park Hotel on Friday, 18 July, and once Clive had met me to pick up the kids Alexander came to join me for dinner. As ever, he was solicitous and romantic.

'I've missed you, Chrissy,' he said, leaning over the table and taking my hands. Later, as I lay entwined in his arms, I felt a contentment that I could not have remotely imagined a few months earlier. But the moment was quickly shattered when, out of nowhere, Alexander told me he had to go.

'Now?' I asked. It was almost midnight.

'Chrissy, I'm so sorry, but this is the way it is with my job. I deal with the US a lot, and there are things I need to sort out before the end of the working day on the West Coast,' he said.

It was an abrupt end to what had been a lovely evening. I had a hollow feeling in the pit of my stomach as I watched him pull on his clothes and shoes and leave the room with one last kiss on my forehead.

Ten minutes later, my phone rang. It was Alexander.

'I really am so sorry, Chrissy,' he said. 'Leaving you there was the very last thing I wanted to do, but it's the way it is with my job. I'll make it up to you tomorrow.'

Good as his word, he returned first thing and took me out for breakfast. We spent the whole day together, walking round Cheltenham, and with each hour that passed the lingering feeling of dismay about his hasty departure the previous evening dissipated.

The love bombing continued from there. On Monday, 21 July, I moved into my holiday let, where, for the first time, I let Alexander meet the children. They took to him instantly, particularly my boys. Alexander had a childlike quality, and he wasn't afraid to get onto the kids' level. He would play on their games console or kick a football around the garden. Then, when the kids went to bed, he would cook dinner, and we would snuggle up on the sofa together.

As he had done from the start, he continued to reflect my tastes back at me: on one occasion he arrived to find me playing an Andrea Bocelli CD I had bought earlier that week, and he became emotional as he said how much he too loved his voice.

Sometimes he stayed over, but on other occasions he would slip away because of 'work', just as he had that first night we had spent together in the hotel. Now, though, I simply accepted it as part of what he did. In my mind, I found his dedication rather poignant. I saw it as the behaviour of some-one desperately trying to prove something in the light of their illegitimacy. Whether he knew it consciously or not, I reflected, I suspected he believed that if he achieved huge financial success his biological father and family might find it easier to finally accept him.

The only thing I found odd was that he never seemed to mention any friends. Whenever he told me what he'd been up to he always seemed to be on his own, but if I asked about it he would laugh it off.

'Don't worry about me, Chrissy, I'm a big boy,' he told me more than once. 'And there's plenty of time for you to meet my friends.'

In fairness, meeting Alexander's extended circle wasn't exactly a priority at that point, as my move date was looming. I had a lot to organise – the rental property in Bishops Cleeve was a furnished let and I had a huge amount to buy and sort out.

After completion, I took Alexander to see the new house. As we walked up the sweeping staircase that led through the property, he told me it was beautiful. 'I can see myself living in this house,' he said.

It stopped me in my tracks. Though I was reluctant to admit it to myself, I had fallen for Alexander hook, line and sinker, but I had had to fight to get out of my marriage and earn some independence again, and I wasn't going to give it up easily.

'Don't go getting any bright ideas,' I told him.

With a laugh, he told me he was only joking. 'I'm just pleased for you, Chrissy. It's a lovely house,' he said.

For the entire duration of our three-and-a-half-year relationship, we never actually formally lived together – though he talked about it all the time. But then, talking was what Alexander did best.

5

THE FIRST CON

Shortly after I had moved into my new home, Alexander telephoned to ask if I was free the next day to meet for a coffee in Stroud.

'Lydia's up from London and she'd love to meet you,' he told me.

I had the kids with me that weekend and a million things to sort out, so it wasn't ideal, but it seemed important to him; I told him I'd make it work somehow. By that point I'd heard quite a bit about Lydia. She was a barrister working in London, although she didn't fully qualify until the following year, and of his two sisters she was the one he was closest to.

And so one Saturday in early August I arrived at a coffee shop in the centre of Stroud with my kids in tow to meet the woman Alexander was already – only half-jokingly – billing as my future sister-in-law. Slim with long black hair, Lydia greeted me with a friendly smile and we exchanged the usual pleasantries as we settled ourselves at our table. She complimented me on how well behaved the children were, then, ensuring that her brother was out of earshot, leant forward conspiratorially and grabbed my hand.

'My brother hasn't stopped talking about you,' she says. 'He's absolutely besotted. I'm so pleased for him – he's worked so hard all his life, but he's never met the right person until now.'

I thought it was a bit strange: it all seemed a bit full on, especially given that we'd never met before, and Alexander and I had only been dating a relatively short time.

Over the course of our relationship, I would spend a great deal of time with his extended family – particularly his step-father Fred, Lydia, Theresa and his mother Philomena, although I didn't meet them until some months after we got together. That said, Alexander was swift to put me in contact with Philomena: not long after we first met, he gave me his landline number, but the first time I rang him I was surprised to hear the phone answered not by him, but by an older woman.

'This is Chrissy,' I said, trying to disguise the note of query in my voice. 'Alexander gave me this number.'

'I'm Alexander's mother,' Philomena replied. 'I'll tell him you called.'

Afterwards, when I mentioned it, he said it was a mistake. 'Look at me – I'm nearly forty and still think I'm living at home,' he laughed.

Speaking to his mother so early on in our relationship did help me start to trust him.

Meanwhile, I noticed that Alexander's living arrangements were pretty unusual. When we met, he lived in Stroud, in a house he claimed to own, with a 'lodger', an attractive brunette named Tracey Spencer and her teenage daughter, Rosie. Alexander told me that he and Tracey had briefly been boyfriend and girlfriend as teenagers and after their break-up had remained close friends. So close that when her marriage had broken down it was Alexander who Tracey had turned to for help to extricate herself from her husband. With little money of her own, she had lodged with him for years, and he had come to look upon her daughter Rosie as his own. The reality could not have been more different.

Was I naive about their set-up? Perhaps, in retrospect, although resigned to the complexities of life might be a better description for it: when you're approaching your forties, you realise other people's lives are complicated. It didn't occur to me to question what they were saying – or at least not then.

In any case Tracey didn't loom particularly large in those early weeks after I moved into my new home: life was too hectic and my focus that autumn was getting the kids settled and into a new routine. My youngest, Sarah, had turned four and just started in Reception at the school her brothers attended, and after dropping them off I would either go to my job at the boutique or have chores to do at home. Alexander would often drop by as I was doing my chores, and we'd have a coffee and chat. Sometimes we'd go out for lunch, and on other occasions he would call on me in the evening once he knew I'd got the kids settled in bed. We'd snuggle up on the sofa, listening to music and chatting, often about Alexander's grand plans for the future.

By then I knew his potted biography reasonably well. What he told me was certainly colourful, featuring a failed marriage in Finland and a government conspiracy to have him jailed. In Alexander's version, after studying at Oxford he'd moved to work in the City of London, where he'd met the Finnish girl who would go on to be his first and only wife. They'd moved to Finland, where he had worked as a mathematical modeller for her father.

'Some of the work was a bit close to the bone, Chrissy,' he told me. 'And that brought me to the attention of the British Government.'

On his return to the UK, he had tried to set up a commercial property venture in Italy but had lost a substantial sum of money when investors pulled out. 'We're talking a couple of million, Chrissy,' he said.

Extraordinary as what he told me was, none of it seemed overly outlandish. Alexander was unlike anyone I'd ever met before – full of big ideas and plans. He seemed to live his life on an entirely different plane to anyone else.

Alexander was certainly a whirlwind. He'd always just come from somewhere or had somewhere to go. On the evenings when he came over once the kids were asleep, we would make love, but he would never stay overnight. There was always something he had to do – an essay to write, an assessment to finish. And so he would soon roll over, kiss me on the lips, tell me he loved me and that he'd call me tomorrow. It was frustrating and upsetting.

'We're meant to be a partnership, Alexander,' I told him more than once. 'What's wrong with waking up in each other's arms?'

'Don't you think I'd like nothing more, Chrissy?' he would say, grabbing my face in his hands and gazing into my eyes. 'I'm doing this for our future. One day not too far away we'll have all the time in the world to lie around in bed together.'

It was confusing, like an endless game of push-me-pull-you – on the one hand he was always in a rush and forever changing arrangements, calling to tell me he would take me out for lunch, then cancelling at the last minute, saying he'd been called to London. On the other hand, his wooing was relentless: he was constantly talking about marriage and our future.

'I've never met anyone like you, Chrissy. I know I am going to spend the rest of my life with you,' he told me over and over, whether having coffee in my kitchen or walking around Cheltenham.

On other occasions he would turn up with an armful of flowers, or a bottle of Chanel perfume. After the dark days that had characterised the end of my marriage the attention he paid me – when we were together – was overwhelming. Even so, in those early months I pushed back, saying we had only just met and that things were moving too quickly. Alexander was also laying some more specific groundwork. While he never gave me an exact figure, early on he told me that his money was tied up in investments in Switzerland. If he tried to bring it to the UK, it would be liable for vast amounts of tax.

'Our future is over there, Chrissy,' he told me repeatedly. 'That's the goal.'

In the early days I used to humour him whenever he talked about upping sticks. While I wasn't against an adventure at some point in the future, I felt the kids had gone through enough upheaval after the divorce, and my focus was on keeping them settled close to their father.

There was another thing Alexander talked about endlessly, which was his hope of getting into the London Business School. One weekend, towards the end of September, he suggested we take a trip to London when Clive had the kids. We drove down in Fred Hatton's old Renault, borrowed for the occasion by Alexander, and as he headed towards the centre, he said he had something he wanted to show me.

'See that?' he asked as we glided past an elegant white Regency-era building bordering Regent's Park. 'If all goes well then I will be starting there in January. It's going to take a lot of work, but it will be worth it.'

The only fly in the ointment, apparently, was the financial side of things. With a name like Rothschild Alexander said he would never be granted a bursary because people assumed he had so much more money than he did. Initially, though, I took very little notice, even when on one October evening he bounded over the front doorstep and announced he had good news.

'I've just had a letter telling me I've got a place at the London Business School, Chrissy!' he said, pulling me into his arms. 'I've done it.'

It was impossible not to be swept up by his enthusiasm, but as we settled down to drink a glass of the champagne he had brought to celebrate I couldn't stop myself asking exactly what the fees were and how he was going to fund it.

'Don't worry about that now,' he said. 'Tonight, let's just enjoy it.'

As the month progressed, though, Alexander became noticeably more downhearted. He told me he was meeting with assorted charitable organisations who might be able to help with his fees, only to arrive back at my house crestfallen.

'It's the same story every time, Chrissy,' he said. 'However much I tell them I have no family money behind me, they don't believe me.'

Soon, the disillusion turned into apparent panic. 'I need at least £70,000 to pay the year's fees up front and get a car and some new computer equipment and specialist business journals,' he told me. 'I don't know what to do.'

I had a sense he was angling for money, but it was money I just didn't feel I could spare, and certainly not for someone I had only known for a relatively short amount of time. But Alexander had a way of wearing you down. Towards the end of October, over a coffee, I told a jittery Alexander that while I couldn't help him with fees I could sort out some new computer equipment. He was grateful beyond belief, and the next day we sat down together at my old laptop. I bought him £3,833 worth of computer kit – a new laptop and assorted paraphernalia.

'I'm so grateful, Chrissy,' he said. 'I promise you it will all be worth it.' He mentioned that I could have his old laptop for myself, although it never materialised.

Two weeks later, as we nestled together on the sofa, Alexander asked me directly for a loan. 'You know I wouldn't normally ask you this, but I just don't know what else to do,' he said. 'Do you think there is any way at all you could lend me the money for the fees?'

I told him I simply didn't have that amount of money: yes, I had £150,000 in the bank, but that had to last – it was all I had left from my divorce settlement after buying the house. In any case, couldn't he take some money out of his fund in Switzerland? Alexander had an oven-baked answer for that one, arguing that he refused to pay a penny of tax to the British Government because of the terrible things they had done.

One night over supper he proffered another solution. 'What about taking out a small mortgage on the house?' he asked.

I pointed out that it was impossible: while I owned the house, I didn't have a full-time job so no bank would take me on as a customer. Never short of ideas, Alexander then had another suggestion: I could raise a charging order on my house, borrowing the money from a friend who would then have a debt secured against my property.

'You've got plenty of friends with that kind of money, Chrissy,' he told me. 'They just have to lend it to you, then when we sell the house and move to Switzerland they receive the money back as part of the sale.'

On and on he went, telling me that the money was small fry in the grand scheme of things, that he had plenty of savings in Geneva, and that I must never worry about my financial future.

'I'll always look after you, Chrissy,' he told me, clasping both my hands in his. If I'd let him, he added, he would also take on a portfolio for me. He knew I'd made an appointment to see a financial advisor, and said it was ridiculous for me to pay to see someone when he was immersed in the world of investments. He suggested a group of shares, which were fore-cast to grow exponentially, explaining that they would be a good investment. 'It will make me feel better if I know I'm not just borrowing money for the fees, but to help you out too,' he told me.

Alexander was right about my friends. Quite a few had money, including Venetia Williams, a successful racehorse trainer I had got to know while I was married to Clive. Generous and non-judgemental, I knew she would gladly help me out, but I wasn't happy at the prospect, believing friends and money were two worlds that shouldn't overlap. Alexander was a master of persuasion, though, and so a few days later I found myself in Venetia's farmhouse kitchen asking her for a £75,000 loan.

By then she had met Alexander, but instead of telling her what the money was intended for I said I was getting a new high-end kitchen fitted and didn't want to take out a costly bank loan. Looking back, perhaps that was an indication that it didn't sit well with me, but either way Venetia didn't question it. 'It's no problem,' she told me. 'I'll speak with my lawyer and get things organised.'

A week or so later, Venetia told me that she had transferred the money. I called Alexander immediately, as he had been piling on the pressure, asking when it would appear and claiming the London Business School were threatening to pull his place. He answered immediately, and suggested we meet at the Cheltenham High Street branch of my bank, Lloyds. But when we arrived, the cashier said the funds hadn't arrived yet. Alexander was agitated and kept asking me to ring her. I felt terribly uncomfortable, keenly aware of the scrutiny of the cashier.

'Alexander, Venetia is doing me a massive favour,' I told him. 'If she says she's done it, the money will be there at some point soon.'

Nonetheless, despite my misgivings, I did call Venetia, who reassured me that the money should land by the following day at the latest. And so it did. With Alexander at my side, I signed a banker's draft – a form of cheque – which Alexander could then deposit in his own account. Together with the near £4,000 I had spent on computer equipment for him, I had now loaned him nearly £80,000.

It was now December, which passed in the usual blur that any parent of young children will recognise. There were endless events at the children's school, and Christmas to organise.

One of the things Clive and I had agreed on when we divorced was that we would try to spend Christmas Day together with the children if we could. This year, the plan was that we would be joined at some point by Alexander after he had spent some time with his own family.

Of course, it didn't work out that way. On Christmas Eve – which also happened to be Alexander's birthday – he arrived laden with gifts for the family, among them computer games and gaming consoles for the boys, a big expensive soft toy for Sarah, and Tiffany earrings, perfume and a Cartier lighter for me. I remember being irritated by the amount he had spent, although it seemed churlish to complain. He told me he would see us all the next day, but as we gathered around the table on Christmas Day I watched as the clock struck first three, then four, then five o'clock.

'What time was Alexander meant to get here?' asked Clive.

'He'll be along later,' I blustered. 'He's got a family event.' But when I called Alexander on his mobile, he told me it was too difficult to get away.

'Mum just wants us all here,' he told me. 'You know what it's like.'

Much later, I learned that he had given his family some expensive gifts for Christmas too. So all in all it was a very happy Christmas for the Hatton family.

6

A BABY ON THE WAY

As 2004 dawned, I was starting to feel increasingly emotionally wrung out courtesy of the endless last-minute cancellations of arrangements – a hallmark of my love affair with Alexander.

He was always in and out – cancelling plans, then turning up when I least expected it. Sometimes I'd come back from dropping the children off at school to find him on my doorstep, announcing that he had some spare time in-between studying. We'd have a coffee at home or pop into town. More than once, he would say he needed to go into Waterstone's to buy books for his course, emerging with a pile of technical business titles that looked like double Dutch to me.

On other occasions he would come to the house with his new laptop and show me how well the shares he had encouraged me to buy were doing. When he'd said he was taking shares out for me I had asked for the contract, only to be told that he'd put them in his Swiss bank for safety. When I challenged him, saying I would prefer to have my own copy, he would act wounded, saying it was hurtful that I couldn't trust him. Who knows what he was showing me on his laptop – I was no expert, but all I *could* see looked like it was heading in the right direction.

One morning over coffee around the start of February Alexander told me that he was wondering whether the London Business School was actually the right course for him after all.

'I've been looking at the Fontainebleau school outside Paris,' he says. 'It has a much more international feel and I think it's worth checking out.'

The following weekend, I left the children with Clive as arranged and we got the Eurostar to Paris, staying in a boutique hotel in the Place Vendôme before catching a train out to Fontainebleau, where we were given a guided tour. Alexander was asking all the right questions, and I caught the eye of the Russian girlfriend of a Finnish man called Aaron Virtanen with whom we had shared a taxi from the station, chuckling at how little sense it all made to me.

Back in our hotel room after dinner at a bistro with our newfound friends, Alexander's mobile phone rang. I could hear a woman's voice on the other line, and it sounded agitated. Alexander took himself into the bathroom where, although I couldn't make out exactly what he was saying, it was clear that he was trying to pour oil on troubled waters. His tone was agitated; he seemed to veer from irritation to attempting to reason with whoever was on the end of the line. When he came back into the bedroom, I asked him who on earth he'd been talking to.

'It's just Tracey. She's just checking up on me.'

'Why on earth would she do that?' I asked. 'She's your lodger, not your lover.'

'That's just the way she is, Chrissy,' he replied. 'She's one of those people who just likes to be constantly in touch. She's on her own with Rosie and she gets a bit het up.'

I didn't buy it – it just didn't feel right. Determined to drill down into their relationship, I kept asking questions, and the more I asked, the angrier he got.

'I've never met a woman who can ask the same question in so many different ways,' he said.

My voice laden with irony, I replied that in that case he couldn't know too many women.

That was it. He stormed out of the room.

Hours passed. I sat on the bed of our hotel room, looking at my clothes hanging in the wardrobe, thinking that I refused to be treated this way for asking questions any woman would ask in the same circumstances.

It was 3 a.m., and I was just about to call reception and ask them to call me a cab to the Gare du Nord when Alexander came back into our room. He was tipsy – I had never seen him like that, as he never drank much more than a glass of wine or one beer – and full of apologies.

'I'm sorry, Chrissy,' he said. 'I shouldn't have left like that. I know the situation with Tracey isn't easy. But after everything that's happened to her, I feel responsible for her.'

We kissed and made up, but the following morning, as we got ready to catch the Eurostar back to England, I told Alexander that if this woman was going to play a part in our future, then I needed to meet her.

'Why don't you invite Tracey and Rosie round for dinner at my house?' I told him. I wasn't particularly mad on meeting them, but as I said to one of my sisters over the phone, I looked at it as bringing two families together.

The evening went well enough: Tracey was friendly and chatty, complimenting me on how beautiful the house was from the moment she crossed the threshold. Rosie seemed sweet too. Tall and tanned with a blonde fringe, she didn't say much, although I couldn't help noticing that she was very clingy with Alexander, who she called 'pappa'. Wherever he was, she wanted to be too: if he sat in an armchair, she would perch at the side.

Rosie seemed to be a typically shy teenager, while Tracey certainly didn't act like a jealous girlfriend. All the interactions I witnessed back then seemed to confirm everything Alexander – and, of course, his family – had told me: that Alexander was the father figure Rosie had needed in the fallout from her parents' toxic marriage, and that Tracey was a family friend.

Back in early 2004 there was another source of tension in my relationship with Alexander. While he showered me with compliments and was incredibly affectionate, he would often suddenly halt in his tracks and tell me that he had better go no further physically as he had to be disciplined about his work. 'Chrissy, we must stop this nonsense now,' he would tease. It made me think that it was a sacrifice for him – I was falling under his control bit by bit.

At the same time, he kept talking about us having a baby – something which, at nearly forty and already the mother of three, was the last thing on my mind. On and on he went, telling me how he was about to turn forty-three and didn't have children, and that the one thing that would make him happy was the woman of his dreams giving him a child.

'Just think about it, Chrissy,' he said. 'We can be a big happy family together. A new baby will bring us all even closer.'

I wrestled with my misgivings night after night. I was in love, but while I loved motherhood, I genuinely thought I was 'done'.

At least I couldn't get pregnant by accident, because after having Sarah I'd had a coil fitted. Alexander used to complain about it, and asked me if I could go on the pill instead, which I didn't want to do for health reasons.

Over time, my refusal to take out the coil became a mounting issue – until fate played right into Alexander's hands. Early in 2004, I developed an infection, which took me first to the doctor's and then on to a gynaecologist. Alexander came with me to the appointment and must have been thrilled when the consultant said that while she thought the infection could be sorted with antibiotics, she would remove the coil as a precaution in case it was an irritant.

'Do be careful in the short term while you work out what you're doing for contraception as I can see you're ovulating,' she told me as I got dressed.

That night, Alexander was strangely amorous, kissing the back of my neck as I washed the dishes. 'If you want to go down that road then you need to wear a condom, Alexander. I don't want another baby,' I told him.

Once more he wore me down. I thought that at my age using no protection just once was surely pretty low risk.

* * *

In April, I spent a few days skiing with Venetia and a crowd of her friends. It had been huge fun, and it was only when I got home that I realised I'd missed a period. Surely I wasn't pregnant? We had literally only had unprotected sex once. I bought a test from the chemist, hoping that on this occasion there was another reason for my usually regular period being late.

To my shock, the unmistakable blue line confirming a pregnancy popped up within a minute. I sat down at the kitchen table, my thoughts racing. It wasn't what I had wanted, but I told myself that maybe this was fated. A part of me was also thrilled to have given the man I loved the one thing he said he wanted.

This wasn't news to be told over the phone, so when I rang Alexander I asked what his plans were and whether we could meet. He must have heard something in my voice, though, as when I said there was something I had to tell him but I wanted to do it in person he wouldn't let it drop.

'What is it, Chrissy? Just tell me.' He must have said it half a dozen times.

There was nothing else for it but to tell him straight. 'I've just done a pregnancy test and it's positive,' I said.

Whatever I was expecting it wasn't what came next, which was total silence.

My stomach lurched. 'Is there a problem?' I asked. 'For someone who was saying how much you wanted a family of your own, you don't sound very excited.'

'I'm just shocked, Chrissy,' Alexander replied. 'I wasn't expecting it.'

'Well, if this isn't what you want then you need to let me know,' I told him, but before I could say any more Alexander told me that someone was at the door and he had to go.

I stared at the phone for the next five minutes. What on earth had I done? I'd gone against my instincts, and now the man who had apparently so desperately wanted a family of his own didn't seem remotely interested.

Twenty minutes later the phone rang. It was Alexander, and this time he was all excitement. 'Chrissy, I am honestly thrilled, it's wonderful news,' he told me. 'I was just so taken aback; I couldn't process what you were telling me. After everything you'd said I thought we might never have a child.'

Of course, nothing with Alexander was straightforward. 'I just want to come and give you a massive hug, but I've got to get to London for a seminar,' he told me. 'I'll be there as soon as I can tomorrow. I love you, Chrissy. This is the start of us being a family.' I felt an odd mixture of relief and disappointment. Relief that he was happy after all; disappointment that once again something so simple could become so complicated.

Whatever I had said to Alexander, it had never crossed my mind to do anything other than go ahead with the pregnancy. I make no judgement on others who make different decisions – every woman's body is her own – but from the moment I knew I had a baby inside of me there was no way I could end that growing life. Alexander came round the following day as promised, bearing flowers, and while I'd asked him to keep the news from his family as I was only a few weeks down the line, he said he was too excited not to share it. He rang his mum moments after he arrived, shouting, 'We're having a baby!' At that point I'd still not actually met her, although we'd spoken on the phone a few times. Every time I asked, he said she wasn't in the best of health, and it wasn't the right time. That all changed when I got pregnant, and from that point on Philomena became a big presence.

Philomena seemed thrilled, trilling down the phone that she hoped it was a boy as she only had granddaughters. My own children seemed to take the news well too. Although he was in and out, Alexander had been a regular presence in their lives for nearly a year, and they all seemed to like him.

There was one shadow hanging over proceedings, though, in the form of my ex-husband. Although he had met Alexander a couple of times when we were handing over the children at weekends, they didn't have a relationship and I knew that he would be shocked by the speed at which I'd got pregnant. I knew I had to tell him in person – it was only right. As we were chatting in the farmyard the next time I dropped off the kids, I said I had something to tell him that I didn't want him to hear on the always-buzzing local grapevine. He was clearly shocked at the news but had the decency to offer his congratulations. 'I hope it works out for you, Chrissy,' he said.

At the time, whatever Alexander's idiosyncrasies and eccentricities, I had little reason to think it wouldn't.

7

A GROWING BUMP ... AND GROWING DOUBTS

One thing was very clear: with a baby on the way, I needed to meet Alexander's parents in the flesh. I'd suggested popping round to their house more than once in the preceding months, but there was always some reason why it wasn't convenient. Now that I was pregnant, however, Alexander seemed to realise that a face-to-face meeting could no longer be avoided.

'They're going to be our baby's grandparents, Alexander,' I told him after he had arrived at mine late one evening, saying he'd returned from a long day of seminars. 'It's just weird that I haven't met them.'

It set the tone for a lot of what unfolded during my pregnancy: when he was with me Alexander was all attention, rubbing my tummy and my feet and telling me how excited he was – but 80 per cent of the time I was home alone juggling three young children and a burgeoning bump.

Eventually, however, Alexander set a date, and one Sunday in early May the doorbell rang and there on the doorstep was Philomena, Fred and Theresa, their biological daughter and

Alexander's half-sister (although, of course, he had told me he wasn't related by blood to any of them).

Paler-skinned and larger-framed than Lydia – who until that point was the only member of the clan I had actually met – Theresa was clad in what I would come to know as her go-to outfit: a rugby top and jeans. Like her sister, Theresa was a barrister, so this rather dressed-down figure who walked into my kitchen wasn't quite what I was expecting, although she was perfectly friendly.

Nor was Philomena as I had imagined. From the way Alexander had talked about her in previous months I was expecting something of an invalid, but while she walked with a stick, she was actually pretty sprightly, and as lunch unfolded it was very clear that she was also the matriarch of the household.

Just as she'd told me on the phone, Philomena made it clear she wanted a grandson. 'I really hope you have a boy, Chrissy,' she said as she helped herself to a portion of the casserole I had made, keen to make a good impression. 'I've already got five granddaughters who I adore, but it would be wonderful for Alexander to have a son.'

By her side, Fred seemed down to earth and gentle. If anything, he seemed a bit hen-pecked, although I would never have said that to Alexander, who came across as a bit of a mummy's boy. I suspect his irritation with Fred boiled down to the fact that he felt possessive about his mother.

No reference was made to the circumstances surrounding Alexander's birth – Alexander had told me it was delicate territory, and it would have seemed vulgar to bring it up.

I was pleased that I had finally met his parents, although it didn't change the fact that Alexander's life remained nomadic, and that he was still living with Tracey and Rosie. While he had spent much of the previous year telling me that he couldn't wait to move in, now, whenever I brought up the subject it was met with endless prevarication.

'It's just not ideal at the moment, Chrissy,' he would say. 'I do most of my studying in the evening when I'm not with you, and it's a nightmare with kids around.' On other occasions he would tell me he felt badly about leaving Tracey and Rosie.

It was frustrating. Whenever we were together Alexander made me feel like the centre of his universe, but we were about to have a baby and we weren't even living under the same roof!

'You have different priorities now, Alexander – or at least you should have,' I told him exasperatedly one evening in May, when the subject had come up again. 'It's very laudable that you are so protective of Tracey, but I'm your partner now. How do you think this makes me feel?'

Each time it would be the same: Alexander would tell me that he adored me, that he couldn't wait to be a father and that all the sacrifices would be worth it when his studies were done, and we could move to Switzerland. In the meantime, he wanted to do the 'right thing' by Tracey and Rosie.

As ever, he also made certain I saw enough of his family to ensure I felt loved and supported. In early May, we travelled with Fred and Philomena to Theresa's home in Dawlish on the Devon coast and had lunch in a local Harvester. Everyone talked excitedly about the new addition to the family. In moments like that, everything felt normal.

He met my family too. In late spring I took Alexander to my mum and dad's home for Sunday lunch. I only learned later that Dad didn't like him from the word go and had told my mum he thought he was rude and arrogant.

As May wore on Alexander also fixated a new mission: he started to raise the notion of putting my house on All Saints Road on the market, telling me I could invest the money and instead rent a home in Stroud. His logic was this: once the baby came along I'd be closer to Philomena, who could help me out with the kids, and we'd be in a better position to move to Switzerland when the time arrived to start his new job permanently.

On paper this made sense, but nonetheless I wasn't particularly keen on the idea at that stage for a myriad of reasons. I'd been in my home less than a year, I was pregnant and the three kids all went to school in Cheltenham, which was half an hour's drive from Stroud. But Alexander was a master convincer. Whenever we were out and about, he would drive around the Stroud area pointing out houses to rent. 'Please trust me on this, Chrissy,' he would say, cupping my face in his hands. 'It really does make sense.'

In some ways he had got me exactly where he wanted me. I didn't have much headspace. As the weeks wore on, I found it harder and harder to argue and in late July 2004 I placed my home on the market.

By that point school had broken up for summer, and the following weeks were a blur of activities and a revolving door of visitors and guests, including old friends from New

Zealand. Mum came to visit too, and Alexander took us out to lunch. Unlike Dad, she liked him well enough, although she thought he was eccentric. 'He's certainly not like anyone else I've ever met,' she told me once.

A fair bit of time was also taken up with hospital appointments, as Sarah had broken her ankle while staying with her dad, which ended up with us going back and forth to A&E and then the plaster clinic.

Amid all this Alexander was flitting in and out. He told me that he was at the London Business School at least three times a week, sometimes more, as well as occasionally flying to Geneva where he claimed a private bank had offered him a small freelance contract. He was also still talking about Fontainebleau in Paris. Frankly, it was hard to keep up.

Although I had plenty of interested prospective buyers, as September dawned I made the decision to take the house off the market. By now I was more than five months pregnant, and Alexander's endless promises to move in had never come to anything. One night, over dinner, I told him that the house would not be sold until more concrete plans had materialised.

'I'm tired, Alexander,' I told him. 'I just feel you are forever moving the goalposts. One minute you are moving in, the next you are looking for property in Switzerland. It just doesn't feel sustainable. I can't rely on you.'

Alexander was ready with his defence, wounded that I couldn't see the plates he was spinning on behalf of our family. 'This is all for us,' he told me.

By that point I had heard enough. Alexander hadn't even come to my baby scan appointments. For the twelve-week scan he had told me there was a vital seminar he couldn't miss, and he'd made another excuse for the twenty-week scan too. Di had come with me to that one, determined that I wouldn't go on my own, and she didn't hold back with her opinions.

'He's selfish, Chrissy,' she told me. 'Whatever he's doing, there's no excuse for not coming to at least one scan. He keeps telling you how delighted he is about the baby – well, it doesn't look like it from where I'm standing.'

I tried to defend him, protesting that he was putting in twelve-hour days.

'Well, he needs to get his priorities right,' she said.

Now here we were, a few weeks later, Alexander only around 10 to 20 per cent of the time, and Di's words were ringing in my ears. There's no doubt that Alexander's ever-changing whereabouts niggled at me. But with his family providing support, my concerns were often quickly forgotten. Lydia would call to ask how I was and if I needed anything, while Philomena would turn up on the doorstep unexpectedly proffering a food parcel.

'To save you cooking, Chrissy,' she'd beam, handing over a three-tier tiffin box filled with delicious-looking homemade Chinese chicken and vegetables.

'It would be nice to see some more of your son,' I told her on one morning in September, as she decanted her food onto my kitchen counter. I was knackered: the kids had just started back at school with all the accompanying madness of new timetables, and I had barely slept the previous night as the baby was kicking.

'Oh, Chrissy, I know it's not easy,' she told me, putting a protective hand on my shoulder. 'I know my son is unusual. But trust me. He's working so hard towards your future.'

Then one evening in November, Alexander came home in a terrible state, saying that he had messed up. 'I'm so embarrassed, Chrissy,' he told me. 'I've had parking fines and congestion charge fines I've not paid, and now I owe thousands.'

'I don't get it, Alexander,' I told him. 'You say you've got hundreds of thousands in Switzerland. Surely you can bring some of it back? Pay your taxes like everyone else. You're just complicating your life when you don't need to, and you're complicating mine – I'm heavily pregnant and I don't need to feel like I am cleaning up after your mess.'

Over the course of that month I gave him nearly ten thousand pounds in cash, drawn from my savings account.

My family didn't know about the money, but they were growing increasingly concerned that Alexander was not looking after me properly. One afternoon in November, Di telephoned to find me in bed, barely able to move. I had tried to move some furniture and had hurt my back so badly that I had had to stay lying down. To get to the bathroom I had to crawl on my hands and knees.

'Where's Alexander?' Di asked. 'Does he know you're laid up?'

I had to admit that I had called him several times and that he had kept promising he would be with me soon.

'Well, he's taking his time, isn't he?' Di replied.

She was fuming, so I wasn't surprised when I learned that after putting down the phone to me she had called Alexander on his mobile and torn a strip off him. Later, she told me that Alexander had lost his usual poise and returned fire.

'The trouble with you sort of people is, you don't understand what's needed to do the stuff I do,' he'd told her.

It was like a red rag to a bull. 'What do you mean, "our sort of people"? Unless you mean people who have the decency to look after their pregnant partner,' Di told him. 'Unlike you.'

The conversation got very heated until Alexander, no doubt realising that his veneer was cracking, slipped into conciliatory mode.

'You're right,' he told her. 'I know you're only trying to look out for your sister. I'm just stressed, but I'll get over there as soon as possible.'

He arrived a few hours later, full of apologies and holding a bunch of flowers. 'I'm so sorry, Chrissy, I know I've been neglecting you. I'm so focused on our future that I'm not looking after you in the present,' he said, enveloping me in a hug.

Of course, it was all meaningless.

8

BECOMING A MUM AGAIN

With my baby due any time, I was anxious to make sure that Alexander was going to be around for the birth. He was adamant that he wouldn't miss it, and for a short time at least the signs were auspicious: with my due date of 15 December now looming, we went Christmas shopping in Cheltenham at the end of November and had lunch the following day. On both occasions he was all attention.

'I feel like we're at the start of a really wonderful new chapter, Chrissy,' he told me.

I was excited too: Alexander had told me he would definitely move in permanently once the baby was born. So when he told me he had to go to France for a meeting at INSEAD business school at the start of December I wasn't initially overly concerned. The baby wasn't due for nearly two weeks, and Alexander promised he would return after a couple of nights. But while Alexander was gone, my waters broke. I was home alone as the children were at Clive's, but having given birth to three children already, I didn't panic. I phoned Alexander who picked up immediately and told me that while he was now in Geneva, he would make his way back. I spent the following day in the early stages of labour, trying to hold off going to hospital until the contractions kicked off in earnest. I'd phoned Alexander several times, only for him to tell me he was having logistical problems.

'It's a long story, Chrissy,' he told me. 'But I'm doing everything I can. I'll be there.'

It was frustrating but I had other things to focus on: by midnight, with still no sign of Alexander, I was in full-blown labour and phoned for a taxi to take me to hospital, only to find there was a wait of at least an hour as, although it was only early December, the office party season was in full swing and Cheltenham's revellers were all trying to get home.

Gripped by panic – I didn't want to have the baby on my own on the living-room carpet, which now felt like a possibility – I grabbed my hospital bag, threw it in the back of the car and drove myself to the maternity wing of Cheltenham General Hospital, putting my faith in my ability to drive through the waves of pain that were washing over me every couple of minutes.

To my dismay the hospital was every bit as chaotic as the town centre so on arrival I was put in a ward on my own, with a curtain pulled around me, and left to my own devices.

I tried to stay calm: my focus was on safely delivering my baby, but I was getting more and more concerned as Alexander was no longer answering his phone: the last conversation we'd had he'd told me he was now back in Paris and on a Eurostar home. Now the phone was going straight to voice-mail.

At 5 a.m., as the contractions washed over me, I telephoned his landline. It was answered by Tracey, who told me his phone had run out of battery, but he had called her quickly to say I was in labour, and that he had had a nightmare journey from London but was on his way.

I couldn't even begin to process why his last call was to her and not me, but by now I was too far gone to care. All I could do was focus on safely bringing my baby into the world.

At 7 a.m. a midwife came to check on me and told me I was ready to go to the delivery suite. As I walked in, I could feel that the baby was due to arrive any minute.

'This baby's coming now,' I told them, gasping for air between my contractions.

'You're fine,' one of the midwives told me. 'You've got plenty of time. Just hop on the bed.' Marcus arrived literally moments later, a tiny, perfect 6lb 5oz bundle.

'I guess you were ready after all,' the midwife laughed.

'Where's his dad?' one of the nurses asked me as she handed over my son, who I could see had his father's shock of dark hair.

I was too happy to be angry any more. 'He's been in Geneva, but he's on his way,' I told her.

And minutes later there he was, standing at the door of the delivery suite with a giant bunch of flowers.

I was full of endorphins, part exhausted, part elated.

And for a while at least it felt like, finally, we were a family.

Cradling his newborn son, Alexander caressed me, stroked my hair and told me how much he loved me and how proud I'd made him.

We weren't on our own for long: within a couple of hours Fred and Philomena had turned up, followed by Tracey.

It was a bit odd – she wasn't family – but at that point I was so blissed out that I didn't really care. Now, looking back, I wonder what on earth she was doing there.

I left hospital a few days later, excited at the prospect of introducing Marcus to his brothers and sister.

They were thrilled by him, even fighting over who changed his nappies.

For a brief time, it seemed like this might be the new normal I had yearned for. Alexander stayed over, helping with jobs around the house and apparently delighting in father-hood.

He talked about where he would put his things when he moved in, and we discussed converting the downstairs draw-ing room into an office.

It was a snapshot of everything I was hoping for – although there was also a disagreement lingering in the air. We couldn't agree on names, with Alexander favouring pompous ones like Augustus.

Even when we finally settled on Marcus – which Alexander deemed a 'strong Roman warrior name' – he insisted that he should also be given the additional name Nathaniel, appar-ently a tradition for all firstborn Rothschild sons.

I wouldn't hear of it. The surname de Rothschild was embarrassing enough as it was, creating too much interest from others, which I didn't like. Besides, I was determined he wouldn't have his way on this one.

In any case, as the day dawned on which we were due to go

to the registrar's office to list Marcus's birth, with no sign of Alexander – he had disappeared the day before, saying he had to go back to London – I countered my mounting irritation with the fact that he couldn't bring his influence to bear if he wasn't physically present.

Then suddenly there he was, screeching onto my driveway with moments to spare before we were due to set off for our appointment. We continued to row in the car on the way there about our baby's name.

We arrived at the registrar's office twenty minutes later, where Alexander found he had an unexpected ally: as I told her we would be calling our son Marcus Alexander de Rothschild, the registrar also expressed surprise that the name Nathaniel wasn't included.

'It's a Rothschild tradition with the firstborn son, isn't it?' she asked, showing impressive genealogical knowledge.

Alexander was thrilled. 'You can't argue with a registrar,' he told me, flashing the smile that still made my heart melt a little.

Reluctantly, I agreed. Of all the battles to have, this one didn't feel that important now. Marcus Alexander Nathaniel de Rothschild it was.

The rest of December was the usual busy blur of family visits and festivities.

Alexander and I were meant to be spending Christmas Day together, but once more the day dawned with no sign of him.

The previous day, he, Philomena and Fred had come for Christmas Eve drinks in the afternoon before leaving around seven.

'I feel like I should have Christmas lunch with Mum and Dad this last time, Chrissy – this time next year we'll be in Switzerland. But I'll be round as soon as I can,' he told me as he kissed me goodbye.

It didn't feel right: Marcus and I were his family now. Instead, just as we'd done the previous year, the kids and I spent the majority of Christmas Day with Clive.

One memory in particular sticks out. I was in the kitchen, up to my eyes in Christmas dinner, with Marcus in my arms.

Clive came in to see if I needed any help, and I asked him to hold Marcus as I opened the oven door to check on the turkey.

Even now I can remember the tears falling down my face. I was hormonal, of course, but I also felt so let down. Behind me my ex-husband was holding my three-week-old baby by another man, while his dad was nowhere to be seen.

Alexander finally arrived at 7 p.m., laden with expensive gifts that I was too shattered to open. I remember shouting at him that things had to change.

Of course, they didn't. While clearly fond of his son, Alexander was never a particularly hands-on father. He would cuddle Marcus, but all the nappy-changing and feeding was pretty much left to me – especially as he wasn't there much to actually do it.

As January dawned, Alexander told me he was going to be away quite a lot over the next few weeks. He had been headhunted for a job with a private bank in Geneva and was also being tapped up by a business school there, the IMD, to do some academic work.

Time and again I asked him about moving in, and time and again he dodged it.

'At the moment it's just easier the way things are, Chrissy,' he told me. 'I know where I am in my own home, and I am travelling so much it seems silly to move my stuff to yours when we are going to be moving to Switzerland in a few months' time.'

Switzerland remained the carrot he dangled in front of me. One evening he arrived home excitedly declaring that he had found the perfect school for the kids on the shores of Lake Geneva. 'In a few weeks, when you feel more comfortable travelling with Marcus, we can fly out together and take a look,' he told me.

In the meantime, he suggested I telephone them and ask for a prospectus.

At this point I was too tired to care about anything much more than getting through each day. Marcus was an adorable baby, but he wasn't sleeping a great deal, and the effort it took to look after him while shepherding my other three children to and from school alongside all the other extra-curricular stuff was taking every last bit of my energy.

Perhaps that's why, when, towards the end of January, Alexander asked me to provide another large sum, I didn't put up an enormous fight.

His first request was for £20,000, which he said would help buy an almost new Volkswagen Golf that a friend was offering at a good price.

'I'm using Tracey's or my dad's car and it's not ideal,' he said.

And certainly, whenever I had seen him arrive on the drive it was in Fred's old Renault or, on occasion, Tracey's car. I wasn't crazy about the idea of dipping into my precious savings, but I agreed, naively thinking that if he had his own car Marcus and I would see more of him.

I did pause when he raised the sum to £50,000, which he told me was for a PhD at INSEAD – something which seemed a gigantic waste of money.

'Alexander, that's a huge amount of money,' I told him. 'How many courses do you need to take?'

Of course, Alexander had an answer for that: the London Business School MBA could be transferred over to INSEAD, whose PhD course was vital for his future prospects.

We went back and forth for hours. I told him his endless studying was starting to feel self-indulgent and that it was time he took part in the real world. His response was the all-too-common riposte that I had simplistic views on life and didn't understand the world of academia.

When that failed to grab me, his back-up was the sob story about how the British Government had taken everything from him, and that he was determined to rebuild his life for himself, me and Marcus.

'If I invest this time now, Chrissy, then it will pay off in the long term,' he said.

It's hard to explain exactly how persuasive Alexander was – and now that he was the father of my son it was even harder to circumnavigate his arguments. After wrestling with it for several days, I told him I would help.

I did try to insist on one thing, however: I said that if I was to assist him, I really needed something drawn up legally. 'We're not married, Alexander. If anything happens to you, I have no claim on your money in Switzerland.'

Quick as a flash he had a solution to that one: as his flesh and blood, Marcus would automatically have a claim – and besides, he would rewrite his will.

'It will all be immaterial when you are my wife, but I'll do anything that makes you feel better, Chrissy,' he said.

He got his way.

I was now £50,000 worse off, but while my bank account had changed, little else had. Alexander continued to leave me on my own at home for long periods with a tiny baby and three children under eight, sleepwalking through the day.

He had another trick up his sleeve too: he'd taken to ringing me in the small hours when he was away to tell me about his exciting new business ventures.

'Please, Alexander, I just need to sleep,' I told him repeatedly, at which point he would – once again – feign hurt.

'You're the first person I want to tell about this stuff, Chrissy,' he'd say.

I felt permanently wired and on alert.

At the same time, he did just enough to keep my love for him ticking over – turning up unexpectedly and taking me out for lunch or sending me a card full of gushing declarations.

And, of course, there were his parents and siblings, who made huge efforts to make sure I felt like part of the family.

'I know you feel like you are second place to his work, Chrissy,' his mother told me one rainy February morning as she cuddled Marcus in the kitchen. 'But Alexander isn't like other men. He's always done things his own way.'

'Just once, I'd like him to do things my way, Philomena,' I snapped. I was exhausted after another sleepless night.

'He's doing all this for you and your family, Chrissy,' Philomena chided.

In reality, I'd almost resigned myself by then to playing second fiddle to Alexander's professional ambitions.

I also had other things on my mind: Marcus had a small health problem and would have to have an operation in March. On paper it was routine, but the thought of my sixteen-week-old son going under the surgeon's knife was keeping me awake at night.

The operation took place at Bristol's Frenchay hospital on 22 March and, once more, Alexander didn't turn up. Instead, he arrived in time to find me sobbing in the corridor outside the operating room, having handed over my baby to a nurse. I knew my son was in the best hands, but any mother can imagine the anxiety pulsing through every vein in my body as I waited for news.

He took me for a cup of tea and held my hand while he told me our son would be OK, which was true, as the surgery went well, although at that moment nothing could quell my worries. 'Nothing bad is ever going to happen to our beautiful boy, Chrissy,' he told me.

I think about that moment quite a lot now. Did he feel anything at all?

The next couple of months were busy. I went to Florida with my sister Di and my children for two weeks, then travelled up to Mum and Dad's for a few days so they could spend some time with their new grandson.

In the meantime, Alexander was ploughing ahead with talk of Switzerland and the need for me to put my house back on the market, and by June he had once more talked me into it.

Today, I still marvel at how he persuaded me. We were in no better a position than we had been nine months previously, when I had taken it off the market because Alexander's will-o'-the-wisp behaviour had made me reluctant to give up my one piece of security. Yet here we were, Alexander still flitting in and out, with a 'For Sale' sign outside the house.

The truth was that I had four children under eight, one of them a newborn baby, and while I was no pushover, most of the time I was too preoccupied, busy and exhausted to question his motivation.

I was also quite excited: the mountains and lakes of Switzerland were a long way from Cheltenham, and it felt like an amazing new lifestyle beckoned for me and the kids.

That said, I knew that it wasn't going to be straightforward. The logistics felt a bit overwhelming, while Clive was understandably concerned about the fact that I would be taking the children out of the UK.

I didn't want to upset him, but I justified it by working out that if they spent the school holidays with his family, it was collectively longer than the alternate weekends Clive had with them at the time.

Alexander was completely unperturbed by any of it – I guess he never had any intention of us leaving the country together. 'We'll sort it out, Chrissy,' he told me.

Later, I learned that Alexander had had his own separate interactions with Clive: he had invited him to dinner at a local pub and then over the meal tried to persuade him to join him on what he claimed was an unmissable property venture, which Clive had pointedly declined. He also asked Clive to be Marcus's guardian should anything happen to us.

One warm evening as I sat in the garden with the children Alexander burst through the door, flustered. 'Chrissy, I need to talk to you urgently,' he said, agitated. I beckoned him to accompany me inside, as I felt like whatever he was going to say was probably best heard out of earshot of the kids.

'I have an £80,000 tax bill. I'm afraid I botched up the tax return and didn't declare my dual nationality. If I don't pay it, I am going to have to move to Switzerland on my own,' he continued. I was taken aback for several reasons, not least because Alexander had told me he didn't pay tax in the UK, while the prospect of him moving away without me was obviously alarming. As ever, Alexander had an answer for everything, telling me that it was a mistake, but that it was better to pay the bill and then claim it back after he'd sorted it all out. Otherwise, he would have to relocate to protect himself, and as I hadn't sold the house, that meant leaving me behind.

I had so much on my plate that I didn't even join the dots, especially since Alexander apparently had many hundreds of thousands in the bank in Switzerland. But then Alexander had a way of bamboozling you with facts and figures, which always sounded incredibly plausible. More than anything I was fraught, exasperated and panic-stricken. Marcus was still tiny, and it felt like yet again all our plans were in disarray.

'I can't give you the full amount, Alexander,' I told him. 'But I can stretch to £50,000.' That was a sizeable chunk of my already diminishing savings left over from my divorce settlement. Once that was gone, I had nothing else to fall back on. Again, I told myself this was an investment in our joint future.

'Oh, Chrissy, you don't know how relieved this makes me,' he told me, enveloping me in a hug. 'I can find a way to get hold of the rest and we can sort it out when we get to Switzerland.'

I honestly thought Switzerland was on the horizon. Certainly, things were moving quickly: days after I put my house on All Saints Road on the market, I had been offered the asking price by the previous buyers who had been disappointed when I'd taken the house off the market the year before.

Meanwhile, I had committed to a short-term rental of a house on the outskirts of Stroud, not far from Fred and Philomena's home, but now a minimum forty-minute drive each way from my life in Cheltenham – which is, of course, exactly what Alexander wanted. This way, I was more isolated, detached from old friends.

The house was lovely, though: detached, with four bedrooms and a stream that ran through the garden, it cost £1,500 a month, which was no small amount given that I'd had to give up work after having Marcus and was now relying on my savings – themselves now seriously dented by the money I had loaned to Alexander. I told him it made little sense to sell a paid-for house and start dishing out on rent, a concern for which he had ready reassurances. 'It's just for a few months, Chrissy,' he told me. 'All these costs will easily be covered when we get to Switzerland – and besides, I'll cover the rent for you.'

I got the keys to the rental house on 25 August 2005 – before All Saints Road had completed – assuming that Alexander would help me with the move. Instead, he insisted he had to be in Geneva, leaving me to supervise the move on my own with four kids.

That was bad enough – but it got even worse when it turned out that the removal men couldn't fit their lorry down the narrow country lane to my temporary new home.

That meant they couldn't unload the furniture or the beds. I had to buy airbeds so we could temporarily camp out, and I spent a chaotic week running between my two homes. It was exhausting, but I turned it into an adventure for the older kids, which they still talk about to this day.

In the middle of all this, meanwhile, was my nephew Mark's wedding at St Ethelwold's Church in Shotton, Flintshire.

Mark was Di's son, and when the invitation had landed on my mat at All Saints Road a few months earlier I had made it clear to Alexander that this was one occasion when he categorically could not mess me around.

'They're not a wealthy family and every place counts, so if you pull out at the last minute then that is costing them money and it's not fair,' I told him.

'Chrissy, I am absolutely going to be there,' he replied.

Then three days before the wedding – on the eve of my move to Stroud – he broke the news about his trip to Geneva.

'I know it's the worst possible timing with your move too, but it's unavoidable,' he told me.

I was furious: this was exactly what I'd predicted.

'Don't you dare even think about not getting back in time for the wedding,' I told him. I was doing the make-up for the bride and bridesmaids and had assumed that Alexander would look after the children.

So you can imagine my feelings when, on the eve of the wedding, I received a call from Alexander telling me he wasn't going to be able to make it after all.

That was it for me, the final straw. He had missed our son's birth, the moment he was taken into surgery, and so much else. I couldn't take it any more and I told him so.

'I'm done, Alexander,' I told him. 'We're through. I'll be in touch when I get back to sort everything out.' I hung up, switched off my phone and cried myself to sleep.

The following morning I piled the kids into the car and drove to Flintshire, feeling utterly deflated. Alexander had left any number of messages for me, but I couldn't even be bothered to listen to them. I was done with his excuses.

Determined as I was not to let my low mood seep into my nephew's big day, Di could obviously see I was feeling agitated, because as I wrestled with some make-up she came over and put a hand on my arm.

'I'm not meant to tell you this as he wanted to surprise you – but I can see you are wound up so what the hell,' she said.

'I've been getting messages from Alexander all morning to say he's on his way back, and while he won't make the church, he's going to see you at the reception.'

It was something, I supposed, although I was still angry. Like it or not, he'd still managed to overshadow a happy day.

From my vantage point in the church, I could see Di constantly checking her phone, which seemed a bit odd: it was her son's wedding after all.

'Everything OK?' I asked as we made our way to the reception.

'Alexander kept texting me,' she told me. 'He was on his way, but he got lost and now his car's broken down and he's waiting for the AA.'

So much for the new Golf. 'Don't bother replying any more,' I told her. 'It's not worth your energy.'

The wedding breakfast unfolded with no sign of Alexander, and by 7 p.m. I decided to go back to our hotel in nearby Hawarden to catch my breath. The evening reception was due to start, but I was exhausted and not sure I could handle it.

As I started to get the kids into their evening outfits there was a knock on the door and when I opened it I found Alexander on the other side.

'I am SO sorry, Chrissy,' he told me, enveloping me in a bear hug. 'You won't believe the day I've had. I'll make it up to you.'

I was exhausted, but now he was here – obviously refusing to acknowledge that I had given him his marching orders – I had an opportunity to show my family that he hadn't let me down after all. We returned to the evening reception, where

Alexander charmed my family and whirled my children round the dance floor.

For a couple of hours all felt well with the world again. At the end, my dad even got on the stage and took the DJ's microphone to thank Alexander for travelling so far to join us. All was forgiven.

This game of happy families didn't last. Once we returned to our hotel room around midnight, I was settling the children into bed when Alexander told me he had to go.

I couldn't believe my ears. 'What on EARTH do you mean?' I said. 'You've only just got here.'

As ever, Alexander was ready with an excuse.

'Chrissy, I didn't want to make you feel guilty, but it was very tricky for me to leave Geneva – I did it because I didn't want to let you down. I've got to fly back first thing, so I just need to get to London and book myself into a Travelodge for a couple of hours.'

So leave he did – although it would be some time before I found out where he actually went.

9

GOING, GOING, GONE

On 9 September I completed the sale of my home on All Saints Road. It had sold for the asking price of £535,000, but after repayment of the combined £75,000 from Venetia, plus interest, alongside assorted other expenses including solicitors' fees, I banked just under £400,000. It wasn't a small amount of money, but it was also all I had left.

That final sum didn't stay in my account for long either. In the run-up to finalising the sale, Alexander had repeatedly told me that I should think about investing as much of the money as possible.

He told me he had a contact at Pictet, a private equity firm, which had a good track record in both public and private investments.

'They tread exactly the right line between caution and risk,' he told me.

I wasn't convinced: I liked my money in a bank. It might not earn much in interest, but nor was it going to be subject to the vagaries of an unreliable stock market, which could go down instead of up.

But Alexander was relentless. 'This is my area, Chrissy. You've said you want financial independence – now here is your chance.'

This was one of Alexander's trump cards: he knew how much I had hated being financially reliant on Clive, and I had told him several times that however much money he had in Switzerland, I would always like my own income stream. At some point in the near future, I wanted to get a job again.

This is what is so clever about serial fraudsters and conmen like Alexander: they find a way of seizing on your insecurities and foibles and reflecting them back at you.

I agreed to pay him £130,000, handed over in two separate bank transfers.

'I'll need to see paperwork,' I told him. In response, Alexander told me his friend Fabia had invested the money at Pictet and had put the documents straight into his deposit account in Geneva.

Understandably I was alarmed by this and told him so. 'This is my money, Alexander. I need to see some documentation,' I said.

'People do this sort of thing all the time,' he told me. 'Remember, Chrissy, this is my world, not yours. It will be fine.'

'Well, this person doesn't do this all the time,' I told him. He promised me that he would find me documentation of some sort, although of course it never materialised.

* * *

One sunny November morning, I took the opportunity of a few free hours to drive into Stroud to do some shopping, and, without even registering it, I found myself driving back through Alexander's tree-lined neighbourhood. While most of our relationship unfolded under my roof, I had been to his house on the odd occasion, but even so I would have nearly missed his house if it weren't for a brand-new racing-green BMW 645 convertible parked on his drive. There it was, shiny and new, nestled next to our Golf.

Who on earth did he know who drove a car that expensive? I pondered.

I asked Alexander that very same question when he arrived at my house that evening – driving the Golf.

He was clearly flustered, although he still managed to come up with an on-the-spot story, telling me that the Swiss bank he was doing some work for had given it to him as a part-payment for work to help him avoid paying tax.

'I guess it's like a company car,' he told me.

'You certainly kept that quiet,' I replied.

'I thought you might not like it as you're very straight, Chrissy,' he told me. 'I didn't want to make you feel awkward.'

Even so, I was irritated. After everything I had done for him, I couldn't help feeling upset that he hadn't thought I might like a spin on the warm summer and autumn evenings we'd had that year.

Meanwhile, he certainly hadn't tried to hide it from his family. Shortly before I'd left All Saints Road and moved to Stroud, Alexander had taken Marcus to a barbecue lunch at his brother Mason's.

I was already booked to have lunch with a friend, and while I was slightly frustrated at missing out on meeting Mason, I didn't want to let her down.

More than anything I was surprised that Alexander had received an invite at all, given that his relationship with Mason appeared prickly to say the least. In the near two and a half years since we had got together, I had never met Mason, despite the fact that he and his wife Anna didn't live far away.

I wasn't sure why, but clearly there was a history between them, although the ever-diligent Philomena tried to ensure that the family got together every now and again, whatever the bad blood. No one, least of all Alexander, seemed terribly keen for me to meet Mason, so I was taken aback to find Alexander telling me that Mason was hosting a 'Grandparents' Day' barbecue and that he intended to attend with Marcus. Nonetheless, it was difficult to argue with his assertions that it would be good for Marcus to meet his cousins – Mason and Anna had five girls.

I now know that while Alexander left from my house in his Golf, he arrived at Mason and Anna's home in his BMW – but he was back in the Golf by the time he returned to see me.

Part of the reason I'd agreed to the sale of All Saints Road and the move to what increasingly felt like the middle of nowhere was that Alexander would be around more – except, of course, he wasn't.

Whenever I challenged him – and this was increasingly often – he now started to lob ill health into the mix, complaining of endless headaches and bugs and that he was suffering from stress.

An email I sent Alexander at the time to the address he was using then – the wordy amarikenderothschild@aol.com – gives a snapshot of how I felt.

'Where do I start?' I wrote. 'How about with the shattering disappointment of your behaviour? Disappointing but predictable. You have no idea how exhausted I am by you. All you ask of me is my understanding and my patience – well, I am afraid you have managed to stretch them to their limits.'

I told him I was sorry about his ill health, but that I was tired of feeling like I was one of only many women in his life.

Alexander's response was to pull all the usual weapons out of his arsenal, bombarding me with declarations of love and apology, but also the usual emotional blackmail.

It was starting to pall: week by week I was starting to get more and more disillusioned and finding it increasingly hard to conceal my feelings from his family.

'I wonder what the point of the move was,' I told Philomena one morning as she sat with Marcus on her knee in my kitchen. 'I'm miles from my friends, I've got a huge round trip to do for the school run every day and he's still barely here. Switzerland still seems a way off too.'

'He's working so hard, Chrissy,' Philomena told me. 'I know it's tough – but it will all be worth it.'

There was certainly no shortage of wider family time. I saw Philomena and Fred quite regularly, while Lydia would phone me often from her home in London. In an effort to make me feel further included, one night in November over dinner at mine Philomena suggested that we take a trip to Chinatown the next day to meet Alexander for lunch.

The next morning, as arranged, she and Theresa arrived to pick up me and Marcus and make the drive into central London, where we parked on the street in Chinatown.

We took a table at a local restaurant and, sure enough, Alexander arrived shortly afterwards with Lydia in tow, looking delighted to see us and announcing he'd taken the afternoon off.

We had a nice enough lunch, then took Marcus for a wander round Chinatown before we started to walk back to the car.

I'd assumed Alexander would be returning to Stroud with us, but instead he said he had to remain in London. 'I've got too much work to do, Chrissy, especially now I've taken a few hours out. I'll stay at Lydia's tonight.' Lydia, Tracey – it felt like everyone had a bigger claim on him than me.

The rest of November was uneventful – what with the endless toing and froing from the kids' school, managing their extra-curricular activities and trying to keep on top of domestic tasks as well as taking care of Marcus, I barely had a minute to think about myself.

One important date was looming, however: Marcus's first birthday. I was determined to throw a party and that this time the entire family would be there – including Mason and Anna. 'It's time I met them,' I told Alexander.

He clearly wasn't pleased, but he didn't have much of a leg to stand on, and a few days later told me they had accepted the invite.

Not for long. The day before the party, Alexander told me they weren't coming after all. It seemed I wasn't going to get anywhere near Mason and Anna.

Not that I had time to think about it, as my main priority was making sure that Alexander didn't miss his son's first birthday party. After all, he was the one who ordered a big cake from Harrods and made a drama about buying all the party food.

'I've got a contact at a local Thai restaurant who is going to do a banquet for us,' he told me.

It wouldn't be my first choice of food for a first birthday bash, but as always Alexander was insistent.

The day of the party dawned, and the guests arrived at midday, as Alexander had requested. Fred arrived with Theresa, my sister Di was there with my friend Lisa, and Clive had come too (it was his weekend to have the children, but they had told him they wanted to stay for the party).

The only person who wasn't there was Alexander. Midday turned to 1 p.m., then 1.30. We were all just hanging around waiting, and I was on the verge of saying that we should all go out when suddenly there he was in the hallway, wielding a mountain of boxes and an enormous cake in a Harrods box.

It was embarrassing, really. Here was a Thai banquet to feed thirty people, when all any of us wanted was a few sandwiches and a slice of cake.

Worse was to come. Only minutes after Alexander arrived, he announced that he needed to go and pick up Tracey and Rosie.

'Since when were they invited?' whispered Diane.

'They weren't,' I told her, through gritted teeth. Alexander must have seen how annoyed I was, as he came over and gave me a hug. 'Rosie doesn't want to miss out – she really does see Marcus as her little brother,' he told me.

Sure enough, he returned with them half an hour later, Rosie wielding a card – in which she had written, 'To my little brother on your birthday' – and Tracey a pair of tiny Timberland boots.

I thought this was odd, as Alexander was always telling me Tracey had no money, and we weren't really friends. But I accepted the gift with as much grace as I could muster.

Only later when Di and I were clearing up did I let rip. 'I'm sick to death of this,' I said. 'I've had it up to here with Alexander being so unreliable, and of Tracey and Rosie.'

I threw Rosie's card into the fire, then put the Timberlands in a charity shop bag and flung them in the boot of my car. I had zero intention of Marcus ever wearing them.

Another Christmas passed with Alexander making only a guest appearance, deploying his usual excuse that his Christmas Eve birthday and the fact that Christmas was a big occasion in his family made it difficult to get away.

I was almost beyond being irritated now and was already thinking about moving out of my new home in Stroud back to Cheltenham. I needed to get my life back, and whatever postcode I lived in it wasn't going to make a great deal of difference to whether or not we eventually got to Switzerland.

December was notable for one other thing, though. Late that month, Fred was taken into hospital after being run over by a car, but when I told Alexander that I wanted to visit he seemed determined for me to steer clear.

I took no notice – I knew Philomena was away, and he was our son's grandfather – so on New Year's Eve I put Marcus in my car, bought a box of chocolates and made my way to Gloucester Royal Hospital.

When I arrived at Fred's ward, I found Mason and Anna at his bedside. It was the first time I had had the opportunity to clap eyes on them, and while Anna smiled warmly, Mason – who actually looked very similar to Alexander – seemed shocked to see me, and promptly turned his back on me before conversing with his wife in French.

Alexander arrived shortly afterwards, and the atmosphere appeared so tense that I didn't stay long. I couldn't really understand why I was feeling all this grief and animosity, but put this latest odd escapade down to the ever-unusual family dynamics.

One thing I did know as the new year, 2006, dawned was that I needed some additional help – I was struggling to manage the lengthy school journeys; many mornings I'd had to strap Marcus into the car just wailing in distress. Happily, help was to come in the form of a wonderful Moroccan lady called Kabira, who worked for a friend of mine as a nanny and was now looking for another live-in position.

'You'll really like her,' my friend Eileen told me over coffee. 'I think she'll make a world of difference, Chrissy. You look exhausted.'

I spoke to Kabira in early January and was instantly reassured by her calm voice and soothing presence. Indeed, over time we would become firm friends – and she would witness much of the oddity of Alexander's behaviour – but as she couldn't arrive until February I had little option but to plough on.

There were periods of normality too. Alexander would come over to spend time with Marcus or arrive in the evening with a takeaway. He was also still taking money from me – relatively small sums, but a thousand here, a thousand there, which once again he would say he needed to pay for X, Y and Z.

Yet there was no question that things were starting to unravel. The arrival of Kabira helped ease the chaos of my daily schedule, but I still felt increasingly isolated and baffled by the direction my life had taken since the early days with Alexander, which had felt so full of promise.

'You say that I mean the world to you,' I wrote to him in another email in March 2006, 'but from my perspective there is no evidence of it. It feels like the only person you really care about is yourself.'

Reading that now, I shudder at how right I was – but back then I was still a few months away from confronting the true horror of who he was.

Towards the end of May he arrived one evening at my rented home and, as we shared a rare peaceful interlude over a glass of wine he said he needed me to draw up a loan document to cover the money I had paid him towards course fees.

'What on earth for?' I asked.

A convoluted tale followed in which Alexander said Her Majesty's Revenue & Customs had seen the incoming and outgoing payments and his bank was asking questions.

'But they must have seen they were going to the London Business School,' I said. 'That can't be deemed an unusual transaction.'

'All I can tell you is that I've been asked to provide a document,' he told me.

Once again, I did as I was asked, as Alexander dictated a document to me, which said I had loaned him money to cover his business course fees.

Funnily enough, he never actually collected it.

By the end of May I had resolved to move away from Stroud into a new property in Cheltenham. Alexander was aghast, telling me that it was mad for me to inflict further upheaval on the kids and that I would be taking myself further away from his family. Of course, in reality, it was a signal that he was losing control. Either way, as I told him, he appeared to be doing his own thing, and now I would do mine.

Other emails from this time show how sad I was about the direction our relationship had taken, yet at this stage I still had no doubts about my money. I think I was struggling so much with the reality of this relationship, which had once held so much promise, that I wasn't allowing my brain to go down that road.

That early summer of 2006 was notable for one other incident: in the middle of June, I was asked if I would like to attend a Father's Day barbecue at the home of Mason and

Anna – the first time I had been extended an invite to their home.

I spent the whole afternoon there, but still I didn't get to spend any time with Anna on her own: we were always surrounded by family. It wouldn't be long until we found our moment.

10

'IS YOUR MONEY SAFE?'

On 23 June 2006 I moved from Stroud back to a five-bedroom house in Eldorado Road in Cheltenham. It had been inhabited by a clutch of student doctors when I first went to view it and was not in the best condition, but it had a sizeable garden and the estate agent said if I took on a tenancy it would be given a lick of paint and an overhaul. I could see that with a bit of TLC it would be a nice family home for however long I needed it.

I moved in on 6 July, again with no help from Alexander, who had flown to the US claiming he had a business opportunity there.

To be honest, I didn't take a great deal of notice of much of what he was telling me now – I had taken the decision to focus on my family until Alexander stepped up to his responsibilities. Nonetheless it was impossible to avoid hearing about another of his new ventures, as not long after I moved back to Cheltenham Alexander told me he was working on a property development business.

He had, he told me, heard of some land that was for sale on the outskirts of the town and said he was in discussions with developers to build high-end green-energy homes in Gloucestershire – something that was relatively forward-thinking at the time.

Naturally it involved some financial outlay to cover architectural drawings and the costs of registering another small company, personalised stationery and the like.

He even commissioned some huge paintings of the houses he envisaged by a local artist called Kevin Blackham at a cost of £3,000 – a cheque I wrote to Kevin directly. 'Who commissions an oil painting of unbuilt houses, Alexander?' I asked him.

'Trust me, Chrissy, it will be worth it,' he told me. 'If we want to reel in the big spenders, you've got to look high end.'

I thought it was bonkers – but then I thought the whole idea was bonkers. Looking back, I can only assume it was another scam to divest decent people of their money, although thankfully he never got to see this one through.

'You've got your studies, you are talking about relocating to INSEAD, you've got a job in Switzerland, and we are meant to be moving there,' I told him one night. 'It's all too much, Alexander; you're spreading yourself too thinly. And I am tired of me and Marcus being at the bottom of your list.'

It was an ongoing complaint.

In fact, by this stage I didn't even want to go to Switzerland. At the same time, I wasn't ready to give up on him – or us. He was the father of my son, and I had become part of his family.

When you have given yourself to something so wholeheartedly you are so invested in it that it becomes very difficult to walk away. I was in too deep, and besides, surely the father of my son wouldn't hurt me intentionally?

By then – and it is devastating to type this – I had handed over nearly half a million pounds, in 'investments', loans and purchases on his behalf, and while I had repeatedly asked to see statements and evidence of holdings, Alexander always told me that the contract notes were held in a safety deposit box in Geneva. 'Don't you trust me, Chrissy?' he would say, time and again. 'You know that all this is for us.'

Maybe so, but in the meantime my bank account was emptying fast. Prior to my move to Stroud, Alexander had promised to pay my rent, but like so many of his promises it had come to nothing, meaning I'd had to find that £1,500 every month myself. Time and again over that spring and summer I said I needed to have some of my money brought back to England. Time and again my words were met with excuses.

Not long after I had moved back to Cheltenham, my phone rang one morning as I was preparing lunch. When I picked up it was to my sister Di.

We exchanged pleasantries for a bit and then Di said she had something a bit odd she wanted to ask me.

'Go on then,' I said, intrigued.

'I can't believe I'm asking you this – but is your money safe, Chrissy?' she said.

It was the last thing I'd expected.

I was shocked that she had asked. No one in the family knew anything about my financial situation.

Di said she knew it was peculiar, but Dad had told her he'd received a message from a spiritualist telling him that some-one in the family was having a lot of money stolen from them.

'It's freaked him out,' she said. 'The only person he thinks it could apply to was you, but he felt funny about asking you directly so he asked me to do it.'

I did feel a flutter in my tummy: I was hesitant rather than a complete cynic about spiritualist stuff – and I'd also been there when Dad had once received some information he could never have known about otherwise.

'It's all fine, Di, there's nothing to worry about,' I told her. 'Maybe it's someone else in the family.'

'Well, that's a relief,' she said, letting out a nervous chuckle.

Still, it unnerved me enough that when Alexander came round the next day I told him I needed to see paperwork on the Swiss funds.

'I also want my own login on the system,' I told him. 'This is my money, after all.'

He came around the kitchen table to hug me from behind, all charm. 'Chrissy, please don't worry, but I totally understand. I'll bring some stuff back with me from London, but I can't give you online access. It's a special investor portal, so only I can get into it.'

I felt the first pricklings of unease at this, though I did my utmost to quash them. Opening that door was too stressful.

Then, a couple of weeks later, I was invited to Mason and Anna's home once more for the sixth birthday party of one of their daughters.

The children were on summer holidays by then, and I gladly took my own kids along. Mason was never particularly forthcoming, but Anna was friendly enough and the kids got on well.

As before, we had no time by ourselves, but when Anna mentioned she needed to go into Cheltenham the following week I suggested she pop over for a coffee.

'Does Wednesday morning work?' she asked.

I checked my diary and found I had very little on that day. 'It's perfect,' I said. 'See you around eleven, although don't worry if you are going to be a bit early or late – I'll be there most of the day.'

The following day Alexander rang – claiming to be in Geneva – and said he'd heard that I'd invited Anna over for coffee.

'Mum overheard you,' he said.

'And?' I replied. 'What's the problem? I like her, and the kids get on well.'

'The problem is that I've told you what she's like,' Alexander replied. 'I don't want her there.'

'Since when do I act on the instructions of anyone?' I replied, my voice rising in pitch. 'You've got no right to tell me who I can be friendly with and who I can't.'

'If you loved me,' he replied, 'you would respect what I am asking.'

'Well, if you loved me, you would be spending some more bloody time with me, and Marcus,' I said before slamming the phone down.

Our interactions were now like this – testy and fractious.

Wednesday arrived, and so did Anna – followed moments later by Alexander, trying to make out it was a spur-of-the-moment visit as he was in the area.

It was pathetic, really. I knew why he was there – it was clear by now after the frequent references to Anna's 'troublemaking' proclivities that he was unsettled about us spending time on our own together, although at that stage I had no idea that his concerns were rooted in a very specific anxiety.

Anna left a couple of hours later after what proved to be a rather awkward get-together. Alexander was noticeably twitchy and left when she did, making any pretence that he was there for any reason other than to supervise us a total sham.

Later, over the phone, I asked him what on earth it was all about. I wasn't even cross now, just half baffled, half amused at being babysat during a coffee with a sister-in-law.

'I've told you, Chrissy, I don't trust her,' he told me. 'I honestly would prefer you not to be friends with her.'

It wouldn't be long before I found out why.

In early August Mum came to stay for a week, and all seven of her siblings came over for dinner one evening along with Fred and Philomena. It was a pleasant enough gathering, although later Kabira told me she'd had an odd exchange with Philomena.

Kabira had seen enough of Alexander to know that she didn't like the way he was treating me. (Later, she told me that he had turned up on more than one occasion when he knew I would be out and taken Marcus to his mother's house in his car, despite Kabira's protestations that it was unsafe because he didn't have a car seat.)

At my gathering that night, Kabira had mentioned to Philomena in as sensitive a way as she could that she knew I would love to see more of Alexander.

'All my children are hard workers, Kabira. That is just the

way they are,' she had told her, before walking away. Kabira thought it was a strange response.

Around a week later, Alexander held a trial presentation to practise attracting investment in his fledgling property business. The £3,000 worth of paintings of the proposed development were on display around my living room, and among those invited to hear his pitch – alongside Fred and Philomena – were my Uncle Tim, as he worked in property, my longstanding friend Eileen, who had a keen head for business, and Sarah Daley, a mum from the kids' school, who was also very successful.

To say the whole thing was excruciating is an understatement: it was certainly like no business presentation I had ever seen. Alexander was sweating profusely throughout and stammered his way through the questions from the floor, which he clearly couldn't address. Sarah Daley in particular was relentless about the funding model and it became abundantly clear that Alexander was way out of his depth.

Afterwards, as I cleared away the plates and glasses after bidding our guests an awkward farewell, I tried to make a joke of it to lighten the mood. Frankly, I was so embarrassed by his presentation that I was wondering what on earth had just happened.

'I hope you've not covered presentations in your course yet, Alexander, otherwise I would be asking for my money back,' I said.

'That friend of yours thinks she's really something, doesn't she?' Alexander said. 'She was deliberately trying to undermine me.'

I remember telling him not to be so ridiculous. In any case, I didn't have time for his hissy fits. I was due to head down to his sister Theresa's home in Dawlish for a couple of days with Marcus. It was Philomena who had suggested I visit, saying Theresa would be delighted to host. Once again, I would be flying solo, as Alexander said he had business to attend to.

It was an odd couple of days. For someone who was 'keen' to host me, Theresa, while extremely pleasant, hadn't really organised anything, and after an uncomfortable night on her sofabed I decided to head home early. I was knackered, and not up to another day of being sociable. Happily, Theresa didn't seem offended, and I set off early to try to beat the traffic.

Arriving on my driveway, I realised I wasn't the only one there: moments after my car pulled up, I was joined by Alexander.

I hadn't told him I was coming home early, so I wondered what he was doing there, especially since most of the time my main challenge was getting him to spend any time in my home at all. Either way, if he was taken aback by my arrival, he hid it well.

'I needed the development paintings to make another presentation,' he told me.

Now I wonder if he had come to take more than that. In recent weeks I had been challenging Alexander more and more about his movements and my money, and now that I had gone against his wishes and moved back to Cheltenham perhaps he felt he was losing his grip. Perhaps he was taking the opportunity in my absence to search through my computer.

I will never know – although by then the chain of events that would end in the collapse of everything I had ever known had already been set in motion: a week earlier, at my son Simon's birthday party, I had once more invited Anna over for a coffee, as she said she had to be in Cheltenham for the day to ferry her children to and from various hockey matches.

Once again Alexander had got wind of the plan, and once again we'd had a series of arguments about it, the latest on the day I arrived home from Dawlish.

Frankly, I was getting sick to the back teeth of it all. And so, the following day, on 27 August 2006, I picked up the phone to Anna to try to get to the bottom of everything.

'Look,' I told her. 'I don't know what's going on in your family. But Alexander really doesn't want you seeing me. There's a lot of tension. Is there something going on I should know about?'

At the other end of the line there was a pause, and then I heard Anna take a deep breath.

'Chrissy,' she said. 'I need to ask you something.'

11

'I HOPE YOU'RE NOT FINANCIALLY INVOLVED WITH ALEXANDER'

The words Anna said next made my stomach drop to the floor.

'I hope you're not financially involved with Alexander,' she said.

Before I had even had a chance to answer, Anna was talking, telling me that Alexander was a serial fraudster who had defrauded an Italian woman called Barbara, and even swindled his brother Mason.

I'd heard about Barbara, an ex-girlfriend of Alexander's who Philomena had mentioned in glowing terms, trilling on about how she had once brought her a present of a beautiful book with a silver cover. Philomena had told me she believed the relationship hadn't worked out as Alexander hadn't been as in love with Barbara as she was with him.

'He was waiting for you, Chrissy,' she had said, smiling.

The story Anna was telling me was very different. While she didn't go into details, according to her Barbara had been another victim who had discovered the truth after Alexander had fled from Italy.

He had also stayed for a time with Mason and Anna in Nottingham and repaid their hospitality by stealing Mason's identity. Mason and Anna only discovered the ruse after realising that they had gone several weeks without receiving any post. After weeks of trying to get to the bottom of it all, they discovered that Alexander had diverted their mail in order to access his fraudulently acquired credit cards, running up a debt of several thousand pounds. Mason had a case to bring against him, but he was persuaded not to go to the police.

Anna told me that their suspicions had been aroused when Alexander had shown up to the Grandparents' Day barbecue in the BMW. Anna told me that Mason had confronted his brother almost immediately – 'I bet Chrissy has no idea about that car' were the exact words she recalled him using. I could barely take it in. I was panic-stricken, my mind racing as I tried to keep it all in. I remember thinking that I had to stay calm, that to lose control would achieve nothing.

I can't remember how the conversation ended; I only recall saying that as she was already due to come for coffee the next day, she could tell me more face to face.

I just wanted to get off the phone, for Anna to stop talking and filling my mind with that madness.

It wasn't that I didn't believe her, but I couldn't handle what she was saying. It was too big, too overwhelming.

I spent a sleepless night tossing and turning, watching the clock go round. Could it be true that the man with whom I had spent three years of my life, and with whom I had a son, was a fraudster? If so, had he stolen from me? I told myself it couldn't be possible – that the father of my child couldn't possibly do that to me.

The next day, Anna arrived with her girls. The atmosphere was peculiar – I didn't really want to hear what she had to say, but I knew I had to, and Anna was more than willing to fill in what she saw as the gaps in my knowledge.

She told me that as well as what had happened with Barbara, Alexander had been in prison in Bournemouth for defrauding a local businessman and then sent to Finland to serve a sentence there for fraudulent activity.

'I think he had only been out of prison a matter of months when you met him,' she told me.

I couldn't take it in. My brain wouldn't let me – it was too big, too horrible. I only knew that I couldn't be hysterical, that I needed to remain calm.

I also knew that I didn't want to share my own financial situation with Anna, who was desperately trying to work out what my circumstances were.

'Have you given him any money, Chrissy?' she asked me more than once.

More than anything I needed to talk to Alexander, although I didn't know where he was. Once Anna left – begging me to look after myself – I must have picked up the phone a dozen times, only to put it down again. I needed to speak to him face to face and I couldn't trust myself not to alert him to the fact that I wanted to confront him with something.

I was sitting on all this turmoil when Lydia rang me later that night, asking how I was. I didn't mention anything to her, but the call ended with Lydia once more telling me how much Alexander loved me.

I spent the following day trying to wrap my head around the scale of the pit I may have fallen into, only for equally shocking news to follow: my sister Di rang to say my mum was in hospital with a suspected heart attack.

It was horrible news, but it gave me one slice of clarity – I needed to park what was going on, get in the car and drive out of Cheltenham to my childhood home.

I spent the next couple of days back in Flintshire. Thankfully Mum's condition stabilised and as August drew to a close I headed back to Cheltenham, feeling confusion descend again as I tried to reconcile what I had been told with what I wanted to believe.

I was just five miles away from home when my phone rang. It was Alexander, wanting to know what was going on and why I had been to see his mum.

I told him what Anna had said about him and asked what I was meant to make of it, at which point he started shouting.

'For God's sake, Chrissy, we all warned you!' he bellowed. 'She's poison. She loves nothing more than to spread her lies.'

I know it sounds silly, but I wanted to believe that she was a liar. Even though it was horrible to think that someone might deliberately try to upset me, it was easier than contemplating the idea that Anna might be telling the truth.

Because it couldn't be true, what she'd said about Alexander. Could it?

* * *

I still had my doubts, of course, and decided to do my own research, googling Alexander's names – and variations of it – several times, only to find nothing. While a few journalists had joined all the dots, the couple of newspaper articles that had been written about some of his exploits hadn't gone online at that stage.

At the time, I found this lack of information reassuring – if he really had done all the things Anna told me he had, then surely there would have been some mention of him somewhere?

I knew I needed to speak to Alexander properly about it. I hadn't actually seen him since Anna had dropped her bombshell, although we had spoken several times since that frantic snatched phone conversation in the car, and I had made it clear we needed to speak face to face.

The opportunity came a couple of days after the family lunch, when Alexander came for dinner. By then he had already been laying the groundwork for more excuses. He claimed he was under tremendous pressure because a business deal had gone wrong, and that he now had reason to suspect that Tracey had accessed his bank account and had been stealing his money.

'I don't want you to worry, Chrissy – your money is safe – but I have got a million things going on at the moment; I am just trying so hard to keep so many plates spinning.'

I quizzed him as hard as I could. Why, I asked him, would Anna tell me these things? Were any of them remotely true?

'Chrissy,' he told me, holding my hands. 'I know we've had some tricky times, but do you honestly think I could lie to the mother of my son about this? I don't know why Anna is behaving like this, other than because she is jealous.'

Whatever he did must have worked: while my mind has blocked out a few of those weeks, I have a memory of writing him an email in which I referred to Anna – to my shame – as 'that bitch' and in another telling him that I had spotted Tracey in town 'strutting around in her designer gear' and that I had wanted to confront her about whether she had stolen from him.

Even as our relationship – and his lies – were starting to unravel, the gaslighting was still apparently working.

Nonetheless, one thing was becoming abundantly clear: I needed money, and fast. My once-healthy bank account was down to the last few thousand, and with my rent amounting to nearly £2,000 a month it wasn't going to last long.

Christmas was coming too, and while I never went overboard on presents, I had four kids to buy for and it all mounted up.

Things came to a head on a bleak, rainy November morning. I'd woken up with a terrible headache, and with a sick feeling in my stomach.

I don't know what made me do it, but I decided I needed to catch Alexander on the hop. I got in my car and drove to his house where, after knocking on the door and seeing his surprised face at finding me on his doorstep, I asked him for partial repayment of my money.

'I've been patient, Alexander, and I've had enough of your excuses,' I told him. 'There must be some way you can get access to my investments.'

What he said in reply took my breath away.

'Fuck off, bitch,' he said, before slamming the door in my face.

I couldn't believe it. The veneer had slipped for the first time, and in the most horrible way. This was an entirely different side to the man I loved, and I could barely stomach it.

I drove home, my mind a whirlwind and my stomach churning.

By the time I arrived home, an email was waiting for me, addressed to 'Darling Chrissy'. He said that he was too embarrassed to call me, but he needed to say how sorry he was.

'It is no excuse,' he wrote. 'But I am under so much pressure and to have more piled on me by the woman I love was too much.'

He asked if I could forgive him, but I wasn't ready to reply to him yet. I sat in the kitchen, my head in my hands, until the key turned in the lock and he came in carrying a huge bouquet of flowers.

'Chrissy, I am so very sorry,' he said, wrapping his arms around me from behind as I sat at the kitchen table. 'I promise you that before the month is out you will have your money.'

What followed can only be described as endless days of buying time. He came over to the house with his laptop, pulling up graphs that showed my investments were climbing. 'If we give it one more week, then that could literally make a difference of £10,000 in terms of what we can get out,' he told me.

On 13 November he came over for a cup of tea, and as he sat with Marcus on his lap, he announced that he was flying to Switzerland the next day to get my money sorted.

'In a couple of days, you will have nothing to worry about, Chrissy – and remember, this is only the tip of the iceberg.'

I had no idea that this would be the last time Marcus would see his father other than on a photograph or via a newspaper report.

It was also the last time Alexander would be in my house. A week later, after days of ignoring my increasingly frantic phone calls asking where he – and my money – was, he arrived unannounced on my doorstep, but he didn't come in.

After backing his car onto the drive he came to the side door, and what he said made me realise once and for all that we no longer had a relationship of any kind.

'I've got a lot of problems, Chrissy,' he said. 'I think it might be a good idea if you stop renting and go and live with Clive for a while until I sort all this out.'

I was flabbergasted, because those words told me in no uncertain terms that he didn't care for me at all: there he was, asking the mother of his son, the woman to whom he had pledged his eternal devotion, to move back in, not with her mum, or a sister, but with her ex-husband.

Now I wonder why he said it at all and didn't just disappear altogether without a goodbye. Was it a tiny last-minute prick of conscience? A bid to help me extricate myself from my rental obligations? I can only speculate. What was clear was that I was being dumped.

'What about my money?' I asked as he walked back to the car.

'You'll get your money,' he said, without even glancing back.

I shouted at him, asking where he was going as he climbed into the driver's seat, but he didn't reply.

Seconds later he was gone.

I went back into the house and sat down, stunned beyond belief. The last three and a half years had been an emotional rollercoaster, which had given me both a beautiful son and dreams of a new life, but also more drama and upset than I could ever have envisaged – and it had all come to this: a flat doorstep exchange in which the man I had once loved passionately had suggested I go back to my former husband.

It was clear this was the end, but what did this mean for my future? Anna's words were now once more ringing in my ears. While I still wasn't able to fully confront the fact that Alexander may have stolen my money, it was clear I needed some clarity.

The next day, I walked into Cheltenham Police Station and said I needed to speak to someone about a possible fraud.

12

THE TRUE AWAKENING

The detective who met me was called DC Arkell, and while she played her cards close to her chest she did listen carefully as I tried to summarise the turbulent events of recent years and my suspicions and fears.

More than anything, I wanted to know if Alexander had a criminal record – because if he did, it would lend a lot more credence to Anna's claims. Alas, DC Arkell was not in a position to tell me, although she said she would look into what I had told her.

The following day I went to Cheltenham to do some early Christmas shopping, desperately trying to distract myself from the million questions that were whirling around in my mind.

It proved to be an auspicious trip. One of my destinations was a book stall, which sold well-priced books that I hoped would provide some good present potential for the children.

The stall was run by a well-spoken, handsome man called Philip Rawlinson, and as the stall was quiet, we ended up chatting for a while. To my surprise, as I turned to go, clutching my purchases, he asked me to go for a drink.

I froze. 'I-I'm in a relationship,' I stammered. I didn't know what else to say – I was so taken aback.

He gave me his business card anyway. 'If you change your mind then you know how to find me,' he said with a smile.

Back home, Kabira was aghast when I told her I'd refused the offer of a date. I hadn't really told her the full story about Alexander yet – I was still trying to process it all myself – but she had seen more than enough to come to her own conclusions.

'Chrissy, just give him a ring,' she said, pointing at my phone. 'I think it will do you the world of good.'

Philip and I met for a drink on Monday, 27 November, in a wine bar in the centre of Cheltenham, and while I hadn't wanted to bring my relationship difficulties to the table it was impossible not to end up unburdening myself about the turbulent events of the previous three and a half years and the financial hardship I found myself in.

Urbane and kind, Philip later told me he was horrified by what he had heard, but, sensing how vulnerable I was, he did his best at the time to disguise his dismay.

Instead, as gently as he could, he said that nothing Alexander had told me really stood up to scrutiny. He was a former investment banker himself, and as a former MSc business studies student he certainly knew that the fees were nothing like the £70,000 that Alexander had suggested.

Philip was also concerned about the amount I had given to be 'invested' in the Pictet bank, and the fact that I had no paperwork, telling me that if the investment existed, he was in no doubt that there would be contract notes and statements to verify the deposit.

I left feeling a maelstrom of emotions: while I had nurtured suspicions about what had happened with the money I had given Alexander for business school, I had only really been able to cope with the deeply upsetting events of the last few weeks by telling myself I at least had some money safely invested somewhere. My focus had been wanting answers about his behaviour.

Now, though, the fears bubbling under the surface – that everything he had told me was a lie – were starting to feel more real.

Thank God for Philip, though. We had only had a first date, but as he hugged me goodbye he promised to help me get to the bottom of things.

The following day I made one of several attempts to contact Alexander and confront him outright about my money, only for the calls to go to voicemail.

As 1 December dawned, I knew that I needed to put my allegations on a more formal footing. Returning to Cheltenham Police Station, I asked once more to see DC Arkell – but this time I was straight to the point.

'I need to report a crime,' I told her.

Once again DC Arkell listened patiently, and took a statement, promising me that she would look into it and get back to me. I also had a crime number. There was no going back now.

* * *

Making things official felt like a significant step forward, but it didn't change the reality of my present-day situation: Christmas was looming, Marcus's second birthday was just a couple of days away, and I was already starting to amass debt on the credit cards that I used to religiously pay off in their entirety at the end of every month.

I knew I had to do something for Marcus's birthday, though – I was doing everything I could to shield all my children from the dramas that were playing out around us, endeavouring to keep life as normal as I could. I resolved to throw a little tea party, inviting my good friends Lisa and Nick.

I deliberately didn't extend the invite to any of the Hattons: as I was no longer in a relationship with Alexander, I certainly didn't feel the need to be in a relationship with the rest of them.

They had other ideas, however: as I cut the cake in my living room on the afternoon of 4 December the doorbell rang, and when I answered, it was to find Fred and Philomena on the doorstep brandishing a gift. They bustled in and took a seat in the living room, apparently completely at ease with joining a party they clearly hadn't been asked to attend.

They stayed for nearly two hours, during which Alexander's name wasn't even mentioned – strange in itself, looking back.

We bade each other goodbye cordially enough, and I said I would be in touch, although I had no real intention of contacting either of them in the near future.

I had enough on my plate: aside from the mental energy needed to try to work out what had happened to Alexander and my money, as a mother of four I also had a packed calendar of end-of-school events and Christmas plays to attend, as well as trying to maintain a happy and joyful house for the kids.

It was like being two different people: around the kids I worked hard to be positive, cheerful Chrissy, but when they were at school the other half of me was staring into the abyss, slowly coming to terms with the grim realisation – suppressed for so long – that I had likely been defrauded and that the relationship into which I had thrown my whole heart may have been nothing but a lie. Sometimes I would find myself gazing at my face in the mirror wondering how any of it could have happened.

Meanwhile the police weren't exactly filling me with confidence. I telephoned DC Arkell routinely to see if she had got anywhere with her investigation, and a week or so after I first formally reported Alexander for suspected theft she told me that at this stage her superiors were 'inclined to review the issues as a domestic dispute'.

I was flabbergasted: the only 'domestic' element to this was that I had once been in a relationship with Alexander – although in time he would even deny this altogether, maintaining we had never been more than friends. Either way, if he had taken money from me under false pretences, as appeared increasingly likely, then it seemed to me it hardly mattered what the state of our relationship was.

Alas, it seemed the police saw it differently, initially at least.

Clearly I was going to have to do a lot of the work myself, although I now had help in the form of Philip, thankfully. Since that first date we had seen each other regularly, and to my amazement he seemed to have no problem throwing in his lot with this penniless mother.

'I don't feel I have a great deal to offer you, Philip,' I said one December morning as we nursed a coffee in my kitchen. I'd had a sleepless night, my mind churning with worry about my uncertain future, and I felt like a worn-out husk.

'You don't need to offer me anything, Chrissy,' Philip replied, placing his hand on mine. 'This isn't a business deal.'

Unlike Alexander, Philip didn't shower me with grand declarations and gestures, and I liked him all the more for it. If anything, it showed me how ridiculous Alexander had been – an uncomfortable realisation, but one I was having to confront every day.

Meanwhile, Alexander himself was still not returning my calls, and by mid-December I decided to send him an email telling him I had engaged the services of a financial advisor and banker to sort out my financial situation and establish when I would get back the money he had invested for me.

He responded just before midnight in a form I would become increasingly accustomed to in the coming weeks: using short, often ungrammatical sentences, full of random block capitals. They were a world apart from the gentle, well-written texts he had sent me throughout our 'courtship' and I found myself wondering if he had used a dictionary for those.

The emails he sent me now made it hard to imagine he had even managed to get a GCSE in English, never mind been a fabled scholar. Addressed to 'Christine Handy' (no more 'darling Chrissy'), they included claims that I had been the one to offer him help, and that he'd never asked me for any assistance. He wrote that 'Due to the unforeseen. CIRCUMSTANCES' it would take some time to resolve his affairs, but that I would get my 'FINANCES'.

He also said that he regretted my 'offer of assistance', which had placed him in an 'awkward situation'.

Of course, he was buying time, and over the next two days his tone got nastier. He sent several emails accusing me of 'malicious behaviour', being 'irrational' and using Marcus as a weapon – the very last thing I would do. In fact, on the contrary, I had made it clear that whatever the status of our relationship he was welcome to come and visit Marcus at any time, although only under my roof. There was no way I was going to allow him unsupervised access.

I was sick and tired of his histrionics, and on 15 December I sat at my computer and, for the first time, set down in no uncertain terms what I thought.

'I believe you have told me many mistruths,' I wrote. 'Over the last three and a half years you have systematically defrauded me of a substantial amount of money.'

I told him I had gone to the police, that I was seeking legal advice to recover the money and that, if I had to, I would go to the press to avoid anyone else falling victim to his lies.

I said I would be happy to meet him face to face for a calm discussion about reparation, before ending like this: 'All I did was try to help you and build a future together because of our son.'

I felt better for sending it, although I wasn't sure what it would achieve, which, echoing times past, was a phone call from Lydia asking if I wanted to take a walk.

'I've actually got too much on at the moment, Lydia,' I told her, before putting the phone down. I had plenty to say to her, but now wasn't the time.

I had other, more urgent matters to attend to: a couple of days after I sent that email, I started an application for housing benefit, applying for emergency funds from the council, citing the situation that Alexander had left me in. At that stage I was still confident that I would get the majority, if not all, of my money back somehow, but nonetheless it was hard to sit there filling in pages and pages of personal information and reflecting on how it had come to this.

Thank God, I got the benefit money – after sending an inspector round, the council said they would cover my full rent for six months, although after that they would only be able to pay half and I would have to move somewhere smaller. It was a reprieve of sorts because increasingly I felt like I was borrowing from Peter to pay Paul.

'This is ridiculous, Chrissy,' Philip said one evening as we sat at the kitchen table a few nights before Christmas. 'If he really does have your money then he needs to get it to you urgently.'

It was Friday evening, and I was due to travel to Flintshire the following day to see Mum.

'Why don't you just give him a call now?' Philip suggested.

Once again, as I had on so many occasions over the last few weeks, I picked up the phone and telephoned Alexander's number – although to my surprise on this occasion he answered.

Trying to keep things civil, I started by asking him if he wanted to try to see Marcus over the Christmas period.

'You've not seen him for weeks, Alexander,' I told him. 'I'm not trying to keep him from you – you're his father. But you have to see him under my roof.'

The usual mumbled excuses followed – that I had made it impossible for him to come to the house, and that it was unfair that he could not take Marcus to his mother's.

I didn't have the patience for it any more, and quickly changed the subject.

'I need to know when I am getting my money back, Alexander,' I said. 'I have next to nothing left.'

He started shouting immediately, a volley of abuse that could clearly be heard by Philip from his position across the kitchen table.

Seeing him raise his eyebrows, I passed the phone to him.

I could only hear his side of the conversation, and at first it was clear he was getting nowhere: even from where I was sitting, I could tell that Alexander was shouting incoherently.

Amazingly, though, Philip managed to calm him down and I heard him explain that he was trying to help me deal with my financial situation as I was in considerable financial difficulty.

He asked about paperwork relating to my investment and when I could expect the return of my money, as well as trying to discover more details from Alexander about his course at the London Business School.

'It's relevant', I heard Philip say at one point, 'because of the large sums of money that Christine lent you in order for you to attend.'

Once again, I could hear Alexander shouting, before Philip told me he had abruptly hung up. Philip tried calling him back, but he didn't answer.

'What did he say?' I asked Philip.

If I was hoping for something to cheer me up then I was going to be sorely disappointed: sticking to the fabrications he had doled out to me, Alexander had told Philip that my investment was 'complex' and a personal matter between him and the bank. He had insisted vehemently that he was going to start a new job in January and that he would be in a position to commence repayments some time after that – but when asked for details of his new employer he was once again evasive.

'I didn't want to press him any further, Chrissy, as I knew he could hang up at any time,' Philip told me. 'But I have to say, it's not looking good. None of what he is saying really sounds legitimate.'

Deep down I knew this already by now – but Philip's conversation was another nail in the coffin of my hopes that somehow this had all been a terrible mistake.

Meanwhile, an hour later, a lengthy and rambling email pinged into my inbox from Alexander. By turns aggressive and faintly conciliatory, it accused me of abusive behaviour and blackmail, while insisting that he would 'honour our agreement'.

'I HAVE NOT EVER DECEIVED YOU ABOUT MY AFFAIRS,' he ended. 'PLEASE THINK BEFORE YOU ACT.'

13

TURNING DETECTIVE

On the morning of 23 December 2006, I was helping to tidy the back garden of my mum's home in Flintshire when I received a phone call on my mobile from an unknown number.

Answering, I heard a voice at the end of the line introducing himself as Sergeant Garrett Gloyn from Stroud Police.

'I'm calling to tell you that we've received a report of harassment against you from Alexander de Rothschild,' he said.

I felt my stomach lurch: of all the things I had expected in the whirlwind of the last few topsy-turvy weeks, it wasn't this. It seemed Alexander was already playing dirty.

Taking a deep breath, I tried to explain the reality of the situation as succinctly as I could.

'I'm afraid Mr de Rothschild is currently the subject of a criminal investigation,' I told Sergeant Gloyn. 'Early in December I reported him to Cheltenham Police as I believe he has defrauded me of several hundred thousand pounds. You can confirm this by speaking to DC Janine Arkell, who is handling my case. If you want any more information, then you should speak to her.'

There was a pause on the end of the line while Sergeant Gloyn took in what I'd told him.

'Look, at the moment we're not taking this any further,' he added. 'But you need to be careful. I probably shouldn't say this, but from what I can see this isn't a man who is going to let things go easily.'

'All I know is that I haven't done anything wrong,' I replied. 'I've sent an email asking him if and when he thinks he is going to repay the money he has taken from me. It's hardly what I would call harassment.'

My tone was calm, but when the call finished I realised my legs were wobbling. With Christmas so close, I had tried my best to push everything that was going on to the back of my mind, but this was a clear shot across the bows: Alexander was fighting back. It was deeply upsetting, not least because a part of me had honestly thought that once I had gone to the police Alexander would somehow capitulate. At worst, I'd reasoned, he'd disappear; at best he might try to meet me halfway and offer some remedy.

Instead, it seemed he was launching his own offensive, one that felt like another assault on my already fragile emotions. Either way, I resolved then and there that, whatever tactics he used, I wasn't going to roll over and let him intimidate me. I needed answers.

* * *

Back at home in Cheltenham on Christmas Eve, I had just put Marcus to bed and was trying to get my other excited children to follow suit when, at around 7 p.m., the doorbell rang.

Opening the door, I found Lydia and Theresa on the doorstep, their arms full of Christmas gifts. Lydia lived in London, while Theresa had travelled up from Dawlish, so they'd both come a long way to visit me.

'Hey, Chrissy,' Lydia said brightly. 'We've got some presents for Marcus. Is he still up?'

'He's just gone to bed actually,' I told them. 'But I will bring him down so he can come and say hello to his aunties.' My voice was cheerier than I felt. 'I guess you'd better come in,' I added, gesturing inside.

The atmosphere was uncomfortable, but thankfully they didn't stay too long. Once I'd brought Marcus downstairs, enticing him with the promise of unknown goodies encased in shiny wrapping paper, there were a few minutes of increasingly stilted small talk until both Theresa and Lydia said they would leave us in peace.

'See you soon, Chrissy,' they said as they walked down the path.

'Not if I can help it,' I thought as I closed the front door behind them. I remember my hands trembling on the latch: though there had been nothing unpleasant about the encounter, I found it deeply unsettling.

Still, I was determined that they wouldn't blight our Christmas. Philip was coming over for Christmas lunch with his two children, and Clive was joining us too. As with any new partner, Philip wasn't entirely thrilled by this notion, but he understood that it was important for the children.

Happily, the day was every bit as fun as I had hoped. Alexander's name wasn't mentioned, and the day worked so well that, as we sat slumped on the sofa with our bellies full and a room full of exhausted but happy children, Philip suggested we repeat it again the following day, and I readily agreed. The kids got on really well and after everything I'd been through it was wonderful to spend some time not feeling permanently on edge.

The kids and I had a relatively uneventful few days between Christmas and New Year, and on New Year's Eve Philip and his kids came over again. This time, though, Philip had a suggestion: we should go into the new year in the spirit in which we meant to go on.

'Let's really start digging around on this guy, Chrissy,' he told me. 'I want to work out how he operates and try to get inside his head. It's the best thing we can do to prepare ourselves for the months ahead.'

Together, we started to draw up an action plan: we would start with Philip writing to Alexander to officially request that he give me the money back, the start of what Philip thought was an important paper trail.

'We also need to work out exactly where he is at the moment,' Philip said. 'And we need to instruct a solicitor.'

And so, once the New Year holiday was over, I made an appointment with a solicitor who had been recommended by a friend. His name was Conrad Gadd, and while he was a criminal lawyer, he normally worked on the defence side of things. Both Philip and I felt this might come in useful – as a man accustomed to giving advice to people who may have been on the wrong side of the law, we believed he would have some interesting insights into the criminal mind.

Affable and worldly, Conrad was a New Zealander who had lived in the UK for many years, and I immediately felt at ease in his company as I took a seat in his comfortable office with its lovely view of Cheltenham.

As I had hoped, Conrad proved very helpful when it came to working out the best way for me to proceed, and I listened intently as he spelled out the options available to me.

Among them was applying for a bankruptcy petition for Alexander. 'If that's successful, you can then employ an insolvency practitioner whose job it is to stand in Alexander's shoes,' Conrad told me. 'That means the practitioner has the power to apply for his bank statements, which otherwise you personally won't be able to access because of data protection. It's the only way you can get an insight into where your money has gone.'

I remember the slight out-of-body feeling that gripped me as this conversation unfolded. It was bad enough having to comb through the fine details of your finances during divorce negotiations. Part of me couldn't believe that I was trying to get a full forensic disclosure from a man I hadn't even married.

It was a good start, but I also had a question, specifically about that racing-green BMW, which Alexander had clearly purchased with my money.

'If he still has that car, is there anything I can do about that?' I asked Conrad.

'If you can prove that Alexander used your money to purchase the car then you are legally allowed to have it repossessed,' he told me.

It was enough for me to feel a renewed energy as I left Conrad's office that morning. These might be small initial steps, but they were important and necessary ones on the road to bringing Alexander to justice.

For any of these things to happen, however, we needed to know where Alexander was living so we could serve the necessary paperwork on him when the time came.

And so, after leaving Conrad Gadd's office, I decided to go round to Alexander's house and find out if that expensive BMW was parked on the driveway.

As far as I was aware, Alexander was still living in his house in Stroud on that tree-lined avenue.

But even as I drove up in my car on that frosty January morning I could sense that there was nobody there – and that instinct was confirmed when I got out and walked to the front window. All the furniture had gone, and there were no signs of life at all. Wherever Alexander was, it wasn't here.

The following day I went back to Cheltenham Police to find out how their case was getting on, and to discuss Alexander's potential whereabouts. 'We're still proceeding with our enquiries, Chrissy,' DC Arkell told me. 'There's not much else I can tell you at the moment.'

It was deeply frustrating: a part of me had hoped that once the police were involved things would start to move quickly, but it was becoming clear that this wasn't the case. The legal cogs were turning, and I knew DC Arkell was taking the case seriously, but I wasn't content to sit back and wait to see where it all led. While my emotions remained in turmoil, at my core there remained a steely streak that left me determined not to be a passive victim.

And so, when Philip suggested that he contact Alexander himself by text to enquire about my money again, I readily agreed.

'Whatever we are doing legally, it doesn't do any harm to see what he says when we contact him,' says Philip. 'Worst case: he doesn't reply. Best case: he might incriminate himself further.'

I watched as Philip tapped out a message asking Alexander to let him know what his plans were in terms of paying back the money he had taken. 'It would be useful to get a timeline,' he added.

Neither of us had really expected a reply, but to our amazement Alexander did message back – in the same short, ungrammatical sentences, full of random block capitals, he had used before.

He would pay the money back in instalments, he wrote, and then he demanded access to Marcus on whatever terms he liked, a request he repeated in a phone call.

Philip replied in the only way he could, telling Alexander that he could not possibly conflate the return of the money with access to his son: they were two separate issues.

Alexander hung up – but then an hour later Philip's phone rang again. This time, however, a rather weary-sounding

Sergeant Gloyn was at the end of the line: Alexander had now made a report of harassment against Philip too.

Around the same time Philip also received an apparently conciliatory phone call from Lydia, who said she was hoping that we could talk calmly about the ongoing situation.

'I know it's difficult,' she told him. 'Things have got out of hand. I know Alexander is doing his best to sort out his finances but I'm hoping that in the meantime we can come to an arrangement about Marcus. I know Mum desperately wants to see him.'

Not long after I'd consulted with Conrad Gadd I had visited the BMW showroom in Cheltenham and matched the date Alexander had purchased his BMW with the time I had given him a lump sum to invest for me.

Happily, the staff at the garage remembered Alexander de Rothschild vividly, as he had ordered the car in the summer of 2005 along with lots of extras – but had then stalled for some time when it came to coughing up the £70,000 cost.

I had given him a large lump sum totalling £130,000 to invest over the course of ten days in September that year – and the day after the first transfer, Alexander had trotted to the garage and paid them what he owed. In short, my 'investment' had paid for his car – and left him with some change to spare.

Having consulted a solicitor, I knew that this was all the proof I needed to make a civil claim against Alexander, even if it didn't meet the burden of proof required by the police to start criminal proceedings.

It was another small step in my journey of discovery, but I remember standing outside the showroom afterwards and having to lean against the wall to steady myself, holding back the sobs that threatened to emerge from the back of my throat.

It felt like if I started crying then I wouldn't stop: my head knew that Alexander had serially defrauded me by then, but being confronted with a piece of evidence like this was devastating. This was *my* money, money I had given Alexander in good faith, believing it was helping him with his career or being invested on my behalf and in turn securing our joint future.

He had gazed into my eyes, made countless promises about our family, then walked away and come here and spent it all on a flash car. I knew this kind of thing happened, that there were men – and women – out there who gave no thought to the feelings of others. I just didn't think it would happen to me.

Still, this evidence strengthened my resolve. It might be a small thing, and I was never going to recoup the full £70,000 this way, but I was going to get that car back come what may.

And so, that same afternoon I phoned a private investigator recommended to us by Conrad Gadd. Nigel Antrobus was a registered process server and private investigator who in time I came to think of as 'quiet but deadly'. A solid and professional gentleman, he was exactly the person I needed to try to unravel Alexander's general movements and also establish where the BMW had got to. It certainly wasn't parked at his mum's, and my circuits of Stroud trying to catch a glimpse of it had also proved fruitless.

The first day I employed Nigel, we chatted for a couple of hours over coffee as I filled him in on the bare bones of what had happened and what I was hoping for.

'I might just pop over to Stroud and see if I can find this car,' Nigel told me as he pulled his coat on when our meeting finished.

Less than an hour later my phone rang, with Nigel on the other end.

'I've found it,' he said. 'It's parked two roads away from his mother's house.'

Bingo! I laughed as I ended the call and dialled another, telephoning Cheltenham Police straight away as a courtesy call to tell them this was a civil action, but I was keeping them informed that I had found Alexander's car and intended to get it back.

My next call was to a recovery firm called Yates to ask them to come and collect it. Explaining that this was the result of a civil action and that I had full authority to do so, I gave them the address where the BMW was parked and told them I would meet them there.

Half an hour later, after taking a taxi, I found myself nervously standing on the kerbside of the residential street while a crowd of interested neighbours started to gather. I couldn't shake the feeling that Alexander might appear round the corner and for a while the bravado I had felt just an hour earlier threatened to evaporate. As much as I wanted to enact this small piece of revenge, I was in no way prepared for a nasty scene with Alexander. Glancing anxiously at the end of the road, I could feel the nerves bubbling in my stomach.

All the anxiety lifted, though, as the recovery truck started to hoist the car onto its rear with a satisfying 'clunk'. This was *my* doing. Despite myself, I started laughing.

My high spirits lifted after I hopped into the front cab of the recovery truck and, as the Yates's driver made his way back to my house, telephoned DC Arkell to keep her up to date.

'I've got the car,' I told her. The phone was on speaker, and I smiled as I heard her impart the news to her colleagues to a backdrop of cheers. However slowly their investigation might have been proceeding, they clearly knew what they were dealing with.

There was lots more to do, though: I had to notify the DVLA that I'd got the car, then I had to get a key so that I could sell it, and do everything legally to make sure I was covered.

Nonetheless, it was a good day and one that, looking back, I believe was a turning point for Alexander. From then on, he was on the back foot.

That day, though, just thinking about Alexander's face as he realised his beloved swanky status symbol had been taken away in such a humiliating way was all the boost I needed. That night, Philip and I opened a bottle of wine and chinked glasses as we toasted my small victory. Score: one point for Team Chrissy.

I was also being kept busy with other legal matters: after starting the process online, by 13 February I was at the point in my bankruptcy proceedings against Alexander where I could raise what was known as a statutory demand to him for the money owed me.

This was *my* warning shot – and one he had ten days to respond to. First, though, I had to try to find a way to serve it in person for it to be viable – which is where my private investigator (PI) was kept busy again. Nigel visited various places he thought Alexander might be, but there was no sign of him.

There was still more endless legal back and forth, however, not least when I discovered that Alexander's family believed he had left the country. It meant that ultimately, three months later, in May 2007, I ended up in court in front of a judge clutching a letter from Sergeant Gloyn affirming that Alexander was very much still present in the UK – something he could attest to personally, as Alexander had attended Stroud Police Station to make one of his endless allegations against me at the exact time he was supposedly abroad.

Back in February, however, Alexander was still trying to keep up the pressure from his end, with a volley of letters from his own solicitor – who of course would not disclose the whereabouts of his client.

Much as I knew I was in a strong position with regards to my son, the stress of everything that had happened in recent months was starting to take its toll. A part of me remained in shock at the vastness of Alexander's betrayal, and the scale of what lay ahead of me in terms of trying to get my financial security back was daunting. I had mounting bills, and despite hours spent filling in forms to claim housing benefit, child tax credit and unemployment benefit, my income in no way matched my outgoings and debts. I also had four young children to look after.

At night I would collapse into bed exhausted, only to lie there, wired, watching the hour hand on the clock go round. At times, I would find myself standing in the centre of a room, gripped with a sense of urgency but without a clue why, overwhelmed with brain fog. One morning, as I stared at the bags under my eyes in my bathroom mirror, I noticed I had developed a cluster of small blisters around my mouth and nose.

Philip was concerned too. He was doing his best to support me, but he knew that ultimately only I could really shoulder the burden of what Alexander had done. I know that at times he felt helpless.

'You need to see a doctor, Chrissy,' Philip told me that morning, when I rang him and told him about the blisters that had erupted overnight.

'I doubt they'll be able to do anything,' I told him. 'I suspect I'll just be given sleeping tablets, and there is no way I can take those while caring for my children.'

I was right. While my longstanding GP, Dr Holland, was sympathetic and understanding, there wasn't very much he could suggest other than sleeping pills, although he did refer me to a counsellor they had permanently at the surgery.

'In the meantime, try to see what you can do to ease the stress on yourself,' the GP told me. He meant well, but I could only respond with a wry laugh.

* * *

Not long after I'd been to see the GP, I returned from taking the kids to school to find a black police van and four police cars in my driveway along with an agitated Philip.

He'd stayed overnight the previous evening, and I'd left Marcus with him and Kabira while I did the school run. Shortly after I left, he'd peered out of the window and seen two men yanking the electric mechanism that controlled the door of my garage.

After calling the police, he'd gone out to tackle them, just in time to hear the older of the pair shout, 'Run!' to the younger one, who had not hesitated to follow his orders.

The police were questioning the older man, who had stayed behind and who turned out to be another private investigator – this one hired by Alexander, who had told him the BMW had been stolen.

The police seemed to think the PI had acted on what he had believed to be legitimate instructions. They also thought Alexander had initially accompanied the PI, along with his younger 'accomplice', and had parked in a car up the road to try to see what happened.

All I could do was bide my time, and a week later I smiled as I took delivery of a new set of car keys from BMW to allow me to get in the car, drive it and sell it.

Mindful that I needed to be transparent, I telephoned the police to ask them to attend while I unlocked the car and checked the contents – although if I was hoping to find a couple of hundred thousand pounds in used notes in the glove box then I was to be sorely disappointed. There was nothing in there of any interest at all.

Two days later, I drove to BMW Swindon, whom I had telephoned previously to check whether they would be interested in buying the car after establishing that the Cheltenham showroom where Alexander had made the original purchase were not interested in taking it back.

It turned out I was following in Alexander's footsteps, because when I arrived at the showroom one of the dealers told me instantly that he remembered the car: Alexander had also brought the car in several weeks earlier to ask about selling it, only to stalk off in a huff at the dealer's proffered £37,000.

Several days later, however, he had returned with his tail between his legs asking if he could take the offer after all.

Sadly not, the dealer had said, because in the interim Alexander had wrecked the alloy wheels. He would buy the car, but now for £35,000 instead. Once more Alexander had left muttering about being ripped off – an irony that wasn't lost on me – but it wasn't an offer I was going to refuse: I desperately needed the money to pay my rent arrears and solicitors' fees.

Watching the dealer produce a cheque for an amount that was dwarfed by the money Alexander had taken from me was a bittersweet moment. But it was, at least, a start.

14

A FUGITIVE, HIS LOCK-UP AND HIS LOVERS AROUND THE GLOBE

On 12 March, with the BMW now sold and the money in my bank account, Alexander took things one step further, attending Stroud Police Station in person to make yet another complaint of harassment and to reassert his claim that his BMW had been stolen.

It was a move that proved to be part of Alexander's undoing when it came to the formal bankruptcy proceedings as it directly contradicted claims that he was not in the country at the time and therefore could not be aware of the petition against him.

Meanwhile, the search for Alexander had been continuing without much luck. We did have an address registered to Alexander in legal correspondence regarding access to Marcus, and over the course of February, Nigel Antrobus had attempted to serve bankruptcy papers on him there several times. The first registered letter, posted to him at that address on 12 February, had been returned to sender with the words 'gone away' scrawled across the envelope.

After several more attempted visits, Nigel sent another letter, which said that he would arrive at the property eleven days later to try once again to serve Alexander personally with a bankruptcy petition and that if he failed to be present an application would be made to the court. The letter was again returned.

I did feel like I was fighting fires on all fronts – trying to protect Marcus, trying to get my money back and desperately trying to safeguard my financial future in the short term, for while the sale of the BMW had at least furnished me with enough funds to secure my immediate future, it was a drop in the ocean of the money that Alexander had taken from me.

I was doing everything I could to shore up my limited finances: I'd sold my car and bought a second-hand banger, and by now Philip had moved in, so that helped a bit financially.

Still, it was hand to mouth. Philip had huge financial obligations to his own family, and now he no longer had a corporate job his own funds were limited. We both knew that the emergency housing benefit that covered our full rent would end in June, after which point we would have to find at least half the rent ourselves.

I considered a part-time job, but the reality was that juggling children and the monumental paperwork required to try to bring Alexander to justice was a full-time job in itself. My health was also continuing to suffer. I had insomnia, and endless headaches. Sometimes, as I watched the clock go round, with Philip snoring gently beside me, I would wonder how it could possibly have come to this.

More than anything, I was weighed down with guilt about the children. While I had told all of them early in the new year that I had split up from Alexander – something they accepted without question or upset, with Simon remarking merely that he thought he was 'strange' – I had not told them anything of the terrible legacy he had left behind. I worried hugely about the impact on their future if I could not get my money back.

'Try not to think too far ahead, Chrissy,' Philip told me, as I fretted once more about the consequences of Alexander's decimation of my financial stability. 'One day at a time.'

Philip was a wonderfully reassuring presence on all fronts, in fact, and he had hugely helped to smooth the transition from Alexander's abrupt departure, slotting into my family instantly, as did his children Tilly and Henry, who came to stay most weekends, along with, on occasion, his eldest son Charlie.

A great believer in giving children memories, Philip was wonderful in creating fun times. Even against the turbulent backdrop of what was going on with Alexander, we had some lovely family occasions – walks, picnics and snow days making sledges from old trays.

Nonetheless, while the children appeared to have accepted Alexander's absence from our lives relatively easily, they couldn't help but be aware that something was going on.

'Are you OK, Mummy?' Simon asked me one night, after coming into the kitchen to find me staring vacantly into space.

'Of course, darling. I just have a lot of things to sort out at the moment,' I replied.

'Is this to do with Alexander?' asked Simon. It was the first time he'd asked about him directly.

'A little bit,' I told him, enveloping him in a hug. 'It's not for you to worry about, but it turns out that Alexander wasn't a very nice man.'

Life was certainly not dull. In the middle of all the endless legal and practical dramas, one night in late April I received a phone call from a withheld number.

I almost didn't answer. It was late, and in my experience calls like these were usually spam. Nonetheless, something drove me to pick up the handset and when I did a male voice on the other end asked if he was speaking to Christine Handy.

'This is she,' I replied. 'To whom am *I* speaking, may I ask?'

The man said he was called Alex and that he lived in Oxford before launching into a tirade in which he said Alexander de Rothschild owed him a large sum of money and that he wanted it back – now.

'I don't care how you get it, but you need to sort this out,' said 'Alex' – if that was, in fact, his name.

His tone was menacing, and while my heart was racing, I tried to remain calm as I proceeded to explain to him that I was a fellow victim and that a criminal investigation was underway.

'You can confirm this by telephoning Cheltenham Police and asking for DC Arkell,' I told him. 'I am sure she will be interested in hearing from you.'

I hung up, feeling unnerved. It seemed to me that there was no good reason for the call, not least because I couldn't work out how whoever had called me would have found my unlisted number.

By this stage I couldn't put it past Alexander to get someone to put the frighteners on me, and even if it wasn't his doing, the fact that someone could contact me out of the blue and make threats was deeply unsettling.

The next morning, I rang DC Arkell myself to make her aware of what had happened.

'It may be that this Alex guy gets in touch,' I told her. He never did.

Another month unfolded – frustrating weeks in which I felt my life was on hold pending the court bankruptcy proceedings. My appeals to DC Arkell for more information continued, but there was rarely anything new that she could say.

'It's an ongoing investigation is all I can tell you, Chrissy,' she told me after one agitated phone call. By now it had been six long months since I had first made a criminal complaint, and while plenty had happened at my end, the legal case appeared to me to be no further on at all.

At least the wheels of the bankruptcy proceedings were finally turning. On 16 May 2007 a hearing took place at Swindon County Court at which, given Alexander's repeated attempts to evade being served papers, I was given permission to apply for 'substituted service'.

This meant that in order to show that I had done everything legal to issue notice of the court hearings, I had to go through final attempts – hence 'substituted service' – to alert Alexander to my intentions, writing to him again and advertising in both his local paper, the *Wiltshire and Gloucestershire Standard*, and the *London Gazette*. But he was nowhere to be found.

On 4 July, Alexander was declared bankrupt in his absence, and a date was set a month later for a public hearing, which the bankrupt person is obliged to attend to declare any outstanding money and goods.

I had no expectation that Alexander would attend the hearing in August, although Philomena was there, accompanied by Lydia and Theresa.

It was the first time I had set eyes on any of them for quite some time, but I was determined to remain calm. Alexander had robbed me of a great deal, but I refused to let him take my dignity.

None of the Hattons made eye contact with me as, at my request, the Insolvency Service asked for permission to issue a warrant for Alexander's arrest for non-cooperation.

At the same hearing, Alexander was also made indefinitely bankrupt.

As part of the bankruptcy proceedings, Philomena had mentioned that her son was in the US. If it was true, as I had long suspected, then Alexander was on the run – from bankruptcy, from creditors and from the police, not to mention from himself: a middle-aged man without so much as a name he could truthfully call his own.

It begged the question of not only where exactly he was, but also where all his things were. Alexander was extraordinarily particular about his belongings, and while he may have taken a few designer bits with him to the US (I couldn't imagine him leaving without his Tiffany cufflinks and the Montblanc pen of which he was so fond), there would be plenty he wouldn't have been able to take. I was determined to track these things down and repossess them. They would be a drop in the ocean of what he owed me, but that was beside the point. It would show that I wasn't going to take any of what had happened lying down.

So where was everything?

I was prepared to bet a lot of money that his things would be in storage, somewhere he thought I couldn't trace them. So, logging on to my desktop computer, I typed the words 'storage units Stroud' into Google, and looked at the several options that popped up.

Some I dismissed instantly – I knew there was no way that the fastidious Alexander would take his stuff to some grotty industrial estate – but there was one relatively smart set-up I thought he might be more likely to use.

'It's a hunch,' I told Philip over breakfast. 'But I think it's worth checking out.'

The following morning, after dropping the kids off at school, we strapped Marcus into the back of the car and set out for the storage unit.

Fortunately, while there we were able to confirm that there was indeed a storage unit under the name of Hatton. What we needed to do now was gain access in order to claim the possessions in the name of the Insolvency Service, who could then go on to sell them at auction. I knew this would require a multi-pronged approach and I was well prepared: a couple of months previously, after starting bankruptcy proceedings, I had appointed an insolvency practitioner, who, effectively standing in Alexander's shoes, allowed me to navigate data protection laws, giving me access to Alexander's bank accounts.

When I got home, I researched the name of the owner of the storage company and initially wrote to him to point out that the goods were being stored in contravention of insolvency regulations and that Cheltenham Police had an interest in them under the Proceeds of Crime Act. As such, I sought his assurance that he would inform either me, the police or the bankruptcy trustee if anyone else tried to gain access to the unit.

It was a perfectly reasonable request, but one which the owner did not seem minded to grant: in his reply he said he could make no such guarantees. What's more, he added that he had instructed his employees not to discuss the matter with me, or offer any verbal information concerning the unit.

In some ways it was comical. 'I'm wondering what I have ever done to him,' I said to Philip with a wry laugh as I read the decidedly chilly letter over breakfast one morning.

I replied to him the following day, informing him that I had forwarded his reply to DC Arkell at Cheltenham Police, and that if I suffered any financial loss as a result of his lack of cooperation then I would be seeking legal advice regarding damages.

I then wrote to Alexander's parents and siblings to let them know about my discovery of the unit, as well as contacting the Insolvency Service and DC Arkell, who went along to the storage unit hoping she might be able to see inside by peeking over the top of what she thought was an open unit.

It was completely enclosed, which meant, as she later told me, that she would only be able to get access with a search warrant. Sadly, none was forthcoming: with Alexander now out of the country, it felt like DC Arkell was battling lethargy in those above her in terms of moving her investigation forward.

Nonetheless, overall my approach seemed to work: towards the end of August I received a phone call from the insolvency practitioner telling me that we finally had permission to access the unit.

I immediately called DC Arkell and Nigel Antrobus, and on 31 August they made their way over to the storage facility to see what awaited them there.

On that warm afternoon of the very last day of August, when they finally got access to the storage unit, they found furniture, pendant lamps, textbooks, kitchen equipment, glassware and a host of empty designer boxes, including ones from Cartier, Montblanc, Hermès and Tiffany.

August proved an unexpectedly busy and revealing month on other fronts too. Over dinner one night shortly after the insolvency hearing, Philip and I discussed the fact that it would help my case if others could come forward to share their stories: if he had done the dirty on anyone else in the area, hearing my story might inspire them to come forward and bolster the case against him.

'You won't have been the only one, Chrissy,' Philip told me. 'People like Alexander do this time and time again.'

The following day Philip contacted a reporter called Philip Skelton at our local paper, the *Gloucestershire Echo*, to see if he might be interested in writing a story about what had happened so far. He told him he had a good exclusive story for him, but in return we would like access to his archives to do some research.

Philip Skelton was interested, although he said it would be easier for him to do our research for us, as he knew how the system worked.

True to his word, Philip telephoned later that day and asked if we could meet for a coffee. He arrived at Eldorado Road the following day, a mild-mannered young man in his late twenties or early thirties. I warmed to him immediately as, producing a newspaper cutting, he told me that Alexander was a very interesting man indeed.

Even knowing what I did by then, what he showed me took my breath away. In his hand was a *Daily Mail* newspaper story written in January 1994 by two reporters called Peter Rose and Stephen Wright, setting out an audacious fraud by none other than 'Alexander de Rothschild'. It was flabbergasting to see just how far back Alexander's duplicity went, and it proved to be an excellent starting point for my interview with Philip about my own experiences, which was published in the *Echo* a couple of days later. The following day, it was picked up by the *Daily Mail*. National interest in my story had begun.

Following the collapse of the Iron Curtain, Alexander had approached the Albanian government with a grandiose scheme to open up new opportunities for a country seen to be lagging behind developmentally at the time. He'd unveiled ideas for a leisure complex, including a hotel, a golf course and a marina.

He was so plausible that all manner of accomplished businessmen were sucked in, and in the autumn of 1993 Alexander had held meetings with architects, engineers and designers at some of London's finest hotels and restaurants, from the Savoy to Quaglino's, the Italian eatery favoured by the A-list.

Under his 'de Rothschild' moniker, he had told investors that he was the result of an indiscretion by a member of the Rothschild banking family.

His astonishing scheme – which asked the European Bank for Reconstruction and Development to provide £50 million – was only uncovered when the Albanians wrote to the Rothschild family, only to be told that Alexander's entire story was a fabrication.

The family were so concerned about what they'd heard that they took out an advertisement in the *Financial Times* denying any involvement in the business project.

After that, Alexander had fled to Finland to get up to more of his tricks, leaving a trail of unpaid luxury hotel bills and business debts behind him. He was arrested in Helsinki and charged with thirty counts of fraud, but before he could be convicted he jumped bail and disappeared. In his absence he was sentenced to twenty-one months in prison.

I had to smile; like all the best liars, Alexander had rooted some of his falsehoods in truth: he had indeed been in Finland some years prior to our meeting, and he had indeed been embroiled in trouble – just of his own making.

The story also confirmed what Anna had told me.

None of this changed the fact that reading it felt like a punch in the stomach, especially when I came to the part which said that his name was nothing more than plain old Marc Hatton. Even the name Alexander – the one everyone used – was a construct.

The next day I took the story into the police station, where DC Arkell was equally flabbergasted about the extent and reach of Alexander's fraudulent ambitions.

'It seems he's been a very busy man,' she said with a wry smile.

Not that these revelations made any difference to their investigation, as far as I could make out. With Alexander out of the country and essentially out of their jurisdiction, the case stalled. Luckily I was getting a taste for confronting things head on by now, and I was determined to marshal my feelings and put my anger to good use. If anyone was going to do something, it was going to have to be me.

15

SOME INTRIGUING
TELEPHONE CALLS

Nigel Antrobus had furnished me with a list of everything that had been found in the storage unit and which had now been taken to the insolvency practitioner.

It wasn't just goods: alongside the jumbled chaos of Alexander's belongings was a stack of phone bills, containing a host of international numbers, some of which I recognised as featuring the dialling code for the US. I hoped one of them might provide the answer to Alexander's current whereabouts.

Armed with a cup of tea, I sat down and started to work my way through the list of international phone numbers – six in all. There was one in New York, and one in Florida, California and Texas respectively, another in Germany and one in Geneva.

My opening gambit was the same each time: if someone picked up, I would say, 'My name is Christine Handy and I wondered if you knew Alexander de Rothschild?'

I got lucky on the first hit, after dialling the Geneva number, believing it might bear some relation to the fact that it was the city to which Alexander had first fled earlier in the year.

I was right. The phone was answered by one Emelie Rossier, a shy-sounding woman in what I sensed was her early forties. She said she had known Alexander for twenty years, and while she refused to go into detail about their relationship, she said he had wanted to marry her.

'What happened?' I asked, trying to quell the churning in my stomach.

'I-It didn't work out,' she stammered. She refused to say much more, other than confirming that it was at her home that Alexander had arrived, bearing what she described as 'a lot of luggage' on 18 May.

Two days later she had asked him to leave, although she refused to say why and said that to her knowledge he had gone to stay with a friend in SoHo, New York.

Thanking her, I hung up, my mind a whirlwind. All those trips to Geneva that Alexander had taken when we were together now assumed a new significance. Was he staying with Emelie? I had to assume so.

It was another layer of betrayal, although the extent of Alexander's duplicity was so enormous that it all seemed to blend into one gigantic horror show by now. I hadn't even been particularly surprised when, during a catch-up chat with DC Arkell, I had learned that among Alexander's belongings in the storage unit there was a stack of newspapers with certain items circled, which she told me were 'of interest' to them. She couldn't tell me any details, but I suspected they were the obituaries of rich men who were leaving wealthy widows behind. It was devastating to think that he had viewed me in the same light. And yet I couldn't allow my emotions to distract me from the task in hand, which was trying to track him own.

My next call was answered by a woman called Maria Wouters, a forty-five-year-old Belgian national who was a single mum to five children, living in Florida.

'Oh, sure, I know Alexander,' she said with what I could tell was a wry smile. 'What do you want to know?'

Over the next fifteen minutes Maria filled me in on her own relationship with Alexander. She had met him in late 2005 – when we were very much still together – on Match. com, the dating site, which I soon learnt was one of his regular hunting grounds, and they had struck up a regular correspondence both on the phone and via email.

Alexander had told her he was a successful Swiss watch-maker who wanted to expand his interests into real estate, although he was also trying to establish a business marketing exclusive Swiss watch brand Parmigiani.

They had first met in person in Florida in January 2007 and he had stayed for five days, after which Maria had thrown him out.

'I got the impression quite quickly that he was trying to get money out of me,' she told me. 'He kept telling me that he had a friend who had fallen on hard times and that he wanted to help her, but his money was tied up in Switzerland. I just kept telling him there was no way I could help. With five kids I barely have a cent to my name.'

During his brief time with her, Alexander was clearly on another fishing expedition: posing as a wealthy man on a property search, he had made appointments to see several multi-million-dollar houses, telling Maria that he was looking to start his portfolio.

No doubt he was looking at the wealthy owners, trying to ascertain if there were any rich single women he could charm. Either way, Maria smelled a rat and told me that when one of her kids had found him snooping round her house late at night she had asked him to leave. His parting shot was to falsely accuse that same child of stealing his Montblanc pen.

'Honestly, he's a ratbag,' Maria told me. 'Whatever you have or had going on with him, I hope you're OK.'

Now wasn't the time to go into it, as I had another pressing question to answer: if Maria and Alexander's 'relationship' had ended as quickly as it had begun in January, then who had he gone to stay with in Palm Beach, Florida, in the summer, as the flight manifests I would later come across showed he had flown there from New York on 5 June 2007? It was a small mystery I never did get to solve.

Another number, this time in California, was answered by a female voice who proceeded to slam the handset down when I mentioned Alexander's name, a response echoed in New York when the phone number turned out to belong to an investment company. A number in Germany, meanwhile, went unanswered.

The next call yielded more fruit, however. On this occasion my call to a number in Texas was answered by a pleasant-sounding woman who told me her name was Linda.

A Danish single mum, she had also met Alexander on – guess where! – Match.com. They had corresponded for a while before Alexander had arrived to stay for a few days in the summer of the previous year – the time he had told me he was flying to the US on 'business'.

The 'identity' Alexander had invented for Linda had some crossover with the one he had adopted for me: he had posed as another mature business student and told her he was going to attend New York's Columbia University that autumn.

He had stayed for three weeks, leaving some of his personal effects, presumably to reassure Linda he would return, and taking $3,000 dollars from her, subsequently vanishing without trace and refusing to return her calls.

Linda had got off relatively lightly, although as a single mum $3,000 was still a significant amount for her to lose. 'Those were my entire savings,' she told me, stifling a sob.

Linda had one other interesting snippet to share: while Alexander was staying, she had overheard him on the phone to his mother having a heated conversation during which Alexander shouted that Tracey must not get the keys to his house as she would find his laptops and the game would be up.

'I asked him who Tracey was and he told me she was an ex-girlfriend who had taken the end of their relationship badly and was out for revenge,' Linda told me.

It was clear that I needed to speak to Tracey at some point too – although for now I had other pressing matters to attend to. With my credit card debt mounting, and the council now only paying half my monthly rent, I was struggling to make ends meet and was already in arrears. Much as I needed to fight to bring Alexander to justice, I also had to make sure I could put food on the table for my family.

16

MORE VICTIMS – AND MY OWN CLEVER RUSE

September was relatively uneventful, bar a couple of incidents.

Early in the month, I telephoned Anna and asked if I could see her for a coffee. After a fairly long period of not being in touch, we had latterly exchanged a few phone calls and relations between us were cordial enough.

Mason gave me cause for concern, though – like everyone else in the family he seemed in thrall to his mother, and it had struck me as odd that he was not more on my side.

Nonetheless I thought Anna might be interested to hear about the recent developments, and our subsequent chat over coffee at her house was amicable as I filled her in on the dramatic events of the last few weeks and the battle to get access to the storage unit.

'Actually, we've got some of Alexander's stuff in storage here in our garage too,' she told me. 'I'm not sure exactly what it is or whether it's valuable, but you're welcome to take a look.'

We went over to the garage at the side of their home and there, nestled in a mound of boxes at the back, was a motley collection of DVDs and a few other bits and pieces.

I was about to rifle through them to see if there was anything of value when Mason turned up.

'What's going on?' he asked, his voice clearly on edge.

'Anna was just showing me the stuff you've got in storage for Alexander,' I told him, trying to keep my own voice as even as I could. I had prided myself on keeping a calm demeanour in the face of provocation thus far, and I didn't want to ruin that now. 'I'd like to take a few bits and pieces back, please.'

My attempt was not successful. 'The only people I will release his belongings to is the trustee who has been appointed to oversee the bankruptcy,' Mason told me firmly. I knew that it was pointless trying to argue, especially given he was acting under his legal obligations. 'If that's the way you want to play it, Mason, then so be it,' I said, walking away.

There was plenty of other pressing administrative business to keep me busy too. By now I was getting into considerable arrears on my rent and needed to try to come to an arrangement with my landlady about how to manage things in the future.

I was desperate not to lose our home.

Philip and I were doing our best to raise whatever small funds we could – we'd even resorted to holding car boot sales – but whatever we were making barely touched the sides.

All either of us could do was pin our hopes on healthy sales from Philip's book stall during the Christmas market period, although that would only buy me some more time rather than helping me out of the financial hole I had fallen into – or rather that Alexander had put me into.

'There must surely be some way of recovering the money Alexander has taken sooner rather than later?' I said to Philip one evening as we sat looking over bank statements, wondering how I would get through the next month. I was still clinging onto that hope.

One morning at the start of December 2007, I went to meet Clive back at the farm. We had a few bits to sort out in terms of our children's timetable over the coming months and it was better done face to face.

Our relationship was cordial enough by then, and if Clive had any latent anger about the fact that his divorce settlement had all but vanished into the clutches of a fraudster then he had worked hard to conceal it, for which I was grateful.

What I wasn't prepared for, as we sipped coffee at the kitchen table in his new home, a converted barn, was for Clive to casually mention that he had received a long letter – I won't say from whom – around the time when Philip and I were battling to gain access to the storage unit.

This was entirely news to me.

'Why on earth didn't you tell me at the time?' I asked. 'And what did it say?'

'I didn't tell you because it's all absolute piffle, and I knew it would stress you out,' he replied. 'As for what's in it – well, you can see for yourself.'

He got up and fetched what I could see even from a distance were four densely typed sheets of paper.

Once I'd got it in my hands, I saw the letter was dated 21 August and I sat, aghast, as I worked my way through it.

I'm not sure what I was expecting, but I certainly wasn't ready for this.

The opening gambit was an accusation of 'relentless bullying of the family' from December 2006 onwards as well as an ongoing campaign of harassment, labelling me a 'woman scorned'.

Each paragraph was more breathtaking than the last: the letter stated that the dispute between Alexander and me – or 'Alex' as he was referred to throughout – was a 'civil' matter; it claimed that Alexander had gone abroad in order to get away from me, and that the contretemps between us was to do with 'gift/loan' arrangements.

What's more, the letter suggested, my hostility stemmed from the fact that Alexander had chosen not to live with me during the course of our time together and even claimed that I had had a five-year affair with an old friend from Chester.

This was categorically untrue – this was the old flame with whom I had briefly reconnected *after* I split from Clive, and Alexander only knew his name as I had mentioned him in our early days together when we were talking about our previous relationships. I was enormously grateful to Clive that he had not given this slur a moment's credence.

There was a final *coup de grâce* at the end of the letter, which contained concerns about Marcus and whether the dispute was affecting his relationship with Thomas, Simon and Sarah. It added, 'I hope Marcus, and his brothers and sister, will not be too damaged by the situation.'

By this point I was almost shaking with rage. The only person who had compromised my beloved children's future and their relationships was Alexander with his callous and calculated actions.

Returning home to Eldorado Road, I sat down to write a letter of my own.

I started out by saying that both the original letter and my response had been forwarded to my solicitor and also to DC Arkell of Cheltenham Police.

In my letter, I wrote that it was Alexander who had not only wreaked enormous emotional damage on his son, but compromised the financial security of all my children.

'As for your suggestion that I am a woman scorned, I beg to differ,' I wrote. 'Alexander systematically targeted me, stripped me of my assets, left me with a child and then disappeared, most probably in the direction of his next victim.

'Alexander has destroyed my financial security, as well as that of my four children. I hope in time to recover from his deceptions. My efforts to discover the truth, bring Alexander to justice and recover what assets he hasn't already squandered are as much to do with my psychological recovery as with my need to recover financially.'

I ended by pointing out that the suggestions regarding an extra-marital liaison had been highly defamatory. I felt better for writing it, although I didn't expect it to make any material difference.

I couldn't help but be struck by the date either: it was Marcus's birthday – his third. And at long last, the day after his birthday, I was able to successfully change Marcus's surname from de Rothschild to my maiden name. It had been another lengthy battle, but it was a vitally important one.

I could not change who Marcus's father was, but I could at least take away one key element of his toxic legacy.

Despite this minor victory I was not in a good way as 2007 came to an end. I was still battling insomnia and anxiety attacks, and my immune system was in freefall.

As a result, I got pneumonia a couple of days before Christmas, which confined me to bed for several days. It made for an altogether miserable Christmas, although as ever Philip did his best to keep everyone's spirits up.

As New Year 2008 dawned, however, I knew that whatever my health issues, if I was to get justice and have any chance of getting my money back, I had to up the ante.

The passage of time had made it crystal clear to me that I was effectively on my own – with Alexander out of the country, Cheltenham Police had more or less lost interest, and while the fact that Alexander had been declared bankrupt did mean I could access his bank accounts through the insolvency practitioner and see where my money had gone – on that BMW for a start, as well as flights, hotels and all kinds of designer goods – it didn't necessarily mean I could get it back.

'He's out there somewhere, Philip,' I said one night in early January as we cleared away the dishes. 'And someone knows where he is.'

Even before Philip Skelton had shown us some of Alexander's past criminal activity, Philip and I had both agreed that I was far from his first victim. As we talked about it again that night, I started to hatch a plan.

'We need a major publicity drive,' I told Philip. 'The local press isn't enough.'

The following day I decided to get in touch with Stephen Wright, the *Daily Mail* crime reporter who had written a news report on Alexander's criminal activities all the way back in 1994.

Stephen replied promptly to my email and was fascinated by what I told him when we spoke on the phone shortly afterwards. Courteous and attentive, he said he would look into what I had to say but would almost certainly need to try to contact Fred and Philomena.

'I'd be fascinated to hear what they have to say,' I said, as I remained unsure what exactly Alexander had been telling them.

Very little, as it turned out – as Stephen detailed in the feature he co-wrote alongside fellow journalist Richard Pendlebury, which was published on 29 January 2008, their enquiry had been met with rebuttal by Fred who had maintained that they had 'nothing to do with him' – meaning Alexander – 'any more'.

They also said they had taken out a restraining order on him. 'The whole thing is very upsetting for us,' Fred had told the reporter who had knocked on their door.

In any case it didn't really matter: the story of Alexander's extended criminality was out there, and it immediately generated a lot of interest. A week later, I was booked to appear on both ITV's *News at Ten* and Lorraine Kelly's morning show.

On one level I was thrilled, on another petrified. I was never one for thrusting myself into the spotlight, and there was no bigger spotlight than national television programmes that bookended the working day.

It was perhaps just as well that my *News at Ten* interview never saw the light of day: I was such a nervous wreck that I sobbed throughout. Fortuitous or otherwise, a big news event – I can't remember what – meant that the footage was scrapped.

Happily, my appearance alongside Lorraine Kelly was more successful, and it was also the prompt for another revealing encounter.

As filming was in London, the producers had agreed to put me up in a hotel the night before. By happenstance, Aaron Virtanen was in the capital the same night – the two of us had kept in touch since we'd first met in Fontainebleau three years earlier – and we arranged to meet for a drink.

Over a glass of wine Aaron – who was now a consultant working in Singapore – listened in mounting astonishment and dismay as I relayed the series of dramatic events that had unfolded over the last few years.

'I am so sorry, Chrissy,' he told me. 'What he has done is unbelievable.'

Yet while the scale of Alexander's duplicity had shocked him, Aaron was fundamentally not surprised.

It was then that I learned how Alexander had tried to extract money from him too, supposedly for another pie-in-the-sky scheme to do with importing designer watches.

'Thankfully I declined,' he told me. 'I liked him well enough, but I always thought there was something a bit off about him and I didn't really trust him.'

In some ways what Aaron told me made me feel better: it appeared that when it came to scams, Alexander was pretty indiscriminate in who he targeted: family, lovers, new friends – he didn't care.

Aaron and I parted company agreeing to keep in touch, and the following day I sat in front of the television cameras once more to be interviewed by Lorraine.

Incredibly sweet, she put me at ease before we went on air, chatting to me sympathetically before the cameras started to roll.

My appearance proved significant, in that afterwards the producer of the show called me to say they had received an anonymous telephone call from someone claiming they knew where Alexander was.

'They wouldn't be specific, but they said he was on the East Coast of America,' the producer told me. Sadly, whoever had rung in hadn't left a contact number so there was no way of getting in touch to find out more information.

It was frustrating, but I also had another plan up my sleeve. For the last couple of weeks, Philip and I had been working on a website, which was now ready to go live.

We'd come up with the idea as we were discussing widening our publicity net, thinking it might help to draw out more victims. Anyone who logged on saw a photograph of me, links to photographs of Alexander, and a précis of my story with a plea to get in touch if they could help me locate this calculating conman before he did the same to somebody else.

'Let's hope this gets us somewhere,' I told Philip as the

website finally went live on a chilly day in early February, not long after I had appeared on *Lorraine*.

After everything that I'd been through so far, I didn't think there were any bombshells left. But then, at the end of February, I received a phone call from DC Arkell in which she said she had something she wanted to discuss with me.

'This isn't going to be easy for you, Chrissy,' she said.

My heart sank. What now? Nothing, though, could have prepared me for what I learned next.

'I'm afraid Hatton' – she used his real name – 'is wanted for questioning in relation to the sexual abuse of a minor.'

I remember feeling my stomach lurch, like someone had punched me right in the guts.

'Who?' I asked when I had recovered myself.

'I'm so sorry, Chrissy, I can't tell you that,' DC Arkell replied. 'All I can tell you is that it's a separate case to yours and it's not being dealt with by this station, but over in Stroud.'

I put the phone down, sickened to my core. Even in the morass of bad news that had come in what felt like waves in recent months, this was something worse than I could ever have imagined: that a man with whom I had been in a relationship of some kind for nearly four years could be capable of this.

I instantly felt guilty by association. Had I been harbouring an even worse monster than the one I already believed Alexander to be? I had taken him to my children's school.

I knew that, difficult as it was, I had to try to banish this from my mind. I was struggling to keep on top of everything as it was, and I couldn't carry much more in the way of psychological stress.

Eventually, when I felt ready, I arranged to meet up with Tracey. I realised it would benefit my case against Alexander if I got all the facts about their relationship – from her side this time.

A week later, I sat opposite her in a coffee shop on Cheltenham's Promenade and listened as she told me what she insisted was the truth about her involvement with Alexander.

She confided that, as I had come to suspect, far from being just an ex-girlfriend to whom he had remained close, she too had been in a sexual relationship with him for some years before we met, and that after I came on the scene he had told her I was a rich benefactor who was supporting him by investing in his future. It all started to sink in: why he could never stay over, why he avoided moving in. Tracey and Rosie had even been staying at a hotel just ten minutes from my nephew's wedding; it was to them he'd left in a typical hurry that night.

'I had my suspicions, but he could be so persuasive, Chrissy, and I was frightened of him too. He always said that if I ever left him, he would make me pay,' she said earnestly. 'I had no idea about what he was doing with your money, and I am so sorry to hear about what has happened.'

Tracey told me she had finally plucked up the courage to leave when she learned I was pregnant, but although they had then been apart for a short time, he had wooed her back.

'He kept telling me it was an accident, that you blackmailed him into sleeping with you once, but I knew at that point that he was lying, and I couldn't handle it. But he made it very difficult for me,' she told me. 'At one point he threatened to kill me with an axe if I didn't go back to him. I felt I had no choice.'

All of this was enough to make my brain spiral in a million different directions, although given the bombshell that DC Arkell had dropped on me about the sexual abuse, it also all felt like white noise.

Meanwhile back at Eldorado Road it was hard not to feel dispirited about the progress Philip and I were making in trying to elicit more information about Alexander's where-abouts. I'd asked Tracey if she had any idea, but she insisted she didn't, and while several people did get in touch with us via our website, it was merely to share their own unfortunate stories of being conned and to seek advice on how they should proceed; there was little in the way of leads.

It was disappointing – but then suddenly my website developed a head of steam. At the start of April, I received an email from a man called John Price, telling me that he, too, had been conned by Alexander.

'I cannot tell you how sorry I am that you have gone through hell and back with this person,' he wrote. 'My story is so long, complicated and involved and, like yours, unbeliev-able that there is no room in this email to tell you the whole story. My involvement with this person could fill a book. At this stage I hope you take some strength in the fact that you are not alone.'

John and I subsequently spoke on the phone, where he filled me in on his story. Newly redundant, he had first met Alexander in 1998 in Gloucester. Together with another business partner, Steven Terry, he had gone into business with Alexander, who was posing as a banker with the highly respected bank Merrill Lynch. Together they set up Spirit of Adventure, a kind of events company that specialised in organising red letter days for the corporate market.

He had been entirely taken in by Alexander, who had presented as a debonair investor but who, of course, was quietly fleecing the duo of the savings they had invested in their start-up. In some ways they got off lightly: John and Steven's suspicions were aroused when Alexander's lifestyle became ever more lavish right in front of their eyes.

He started to drive a BMW convertible and took to wearing suits that cost as much as most people earned in a month.

John and Steven realised that their money was clearly funding it and called the police, but by the time they got wise to what had happened Alexander had already taken £60,000 of their money and done a runner.

John had been incensed and was so determined to see justice served that he had personally nailed posters of Alexander around Stroud, until he was eventually recognised by a neighbour and arrested by the police. The judge at his subsequent trial, who jailed him for eighteen months, told him he 'hid behind a façade of pretence and deceit'.

It was a statement you could apply to the whole of our relationship.

When he emerged from prison on 31 December 2002, Alexander was promptly rearrested and sent back to Finland to serve his outstanding jail sentence for his crimes in Helsinki.

Again, it confirmed that when we met in that Cheltenham coffee shop he had been out of prison for just five months.

John could not have been more helpful, offering to contact DC Arkell with his story and provide a statement. 'I can't do anything to change what happened to me, but I will do everything I can to help you.'

In fact, it had actually helped just hearing his story: John was very far from a fool, and the fact that an astute business-man had been taken in by Alexander was proof again of his terrible skills.

John would never forgive him for what he had done and told me that, as far as he was concerned, Alexander was the devil in human form.

Another contact through the website was more puzzling. It came from someone who called herself Sabrina but was enigmatic in tone. She wrote that she lived in America and had been in a relationship with Alexander, which was now over, but she wanted to know more about my back-ground.

Her tone was slightly confrontational, with an edge suggest-ing that I was making things up. When I wrote back suggesting that maybe we speak on the phone she disappeared.

It was frustrating, although it was further indication that Alexander was up to his old tricks on the other side of the Atlantic.

In her contact to the site Sabrina had said she believed he was now in New York – on the East Coast of the US, as the anonymous caller to the *Lorraine* show had suggested a month or so earlier. But New York was a very big place and I despaired of being able to track him down there.

Little did I know that my luck was about to change.

When my eyes flickered open on 7 April 2008 I had no sense at all that it would be anything other than an ordinary day. Pulling on my dressing gown, I headed downstairs, turning on the computer on the way to the kitchen to make coffee. It had become something of a morning ritual since my website had gone live, one of my twice daily or so check-ins to see if anyone had got in touch with significant information.

So far, two months in, I'd received nothing of any real use – but today was different. On my screen were three separate emails, one from someone called Nate, another from a man called Bob, and one from someone called Samuel Ricci.

They turned out, respectively, to be the son, ex-husband and nephew of Julia Tyler, a wealthy fifty-year-old divorcee from upstate New York.

With trembling fingers, I clicked 'open' on the first email, and read the following.

'This man lives at my house with my mom,' wrote Nate. 'Please help me and tell me anything I can do.'

My fingers clicked on the second email, which had also been sent overnight, from Bob: 'I'm sure my son Nate has already sent you an email today, but if not this guy is living in Lincolndale NY with my son's mother. Other than his being in the USA illegally, I don't think he's wanted here for anything. How do you propose to use this information of his whereabouts? What would you propose we do?'

My heart thumping in my chest, I clicked on the third email from Samuel, which was more detailed. In it, he said his Aunt Julia, his mum's sister, was getting 'sucked in'. She had met him on Match.com in July 2004, around the same time I'd put my house on the market the first time. She had flown to the UK several times – presumably while we were still together – and now Alexander was living at her home.

Just as he had with me, Alexander had told Julia that his assets were frozen, and boasted of plans to build a large housing complex all over the world.

'I hate him,' Samuel wrote. 'I am currently trying to have him deported from the country; he is a snake and my family at this point in time does not need any of this. He has successfully driven my cousins from the house so he has the entire house to himself … I am willing to work with you to have him deported, arrested or anything we can have done. Please respond to me. Again, my name is Sam and I feel for you.'

Tingling with nerves, I headed upstairs to give Philip his coffee.

'You'll never guess what. We've found him,' I told him.

Philip sat bolt upright, astonished: I think he had secretly given up hope by this point.

Several hours later, after replying to his email and suggesting it would be good to have a chat, I spoke to Bob on the phone.

A lovely-sounding guy, he gave me a bit more background. He had been amicably divorced from Julia for some years, and had latterly become concerned about Alexander's influence on his ex and the safety of his children. Joe, then twenty, and eighteen-year-old Nate despised their mum's new boyfriend so much that they had moved out of the family home, leaving behind their fifteen-year-old sister, Taylor.

Worried that Alexander's high-octane claims did not stand up to scrutiny, they had decided to google him, only to come across my website.

'We were pretty shocked,' Bob told me. 'I don't think any of us were expecting that.'

I knew I had to be careful what I said. Yet at this stage I felt I couldn't say anything. People carry guns in America, and I had no way of knowing how Bob might react.

Instead, I told him more about my own predicament and my desire to see Alexander brought to book.

He ended by giving me Julia's address.

'She's not going to be happy, but we've got to get this guy out of her life,' he said.

Thanking him, I ended the conversation and turned to Philip.

'We need to tell DC Arkell,' I told him excitedly. This was everything I had been waiting for: the chance to finally reel him in, even if it had meant doing the police's job for them. I rang the station, only to be told that DC Arkell wasn't in until the following day.

I could hardly bear to wait, but it was pointless trying to deal with anyone else, and there was one thing I could do in the meantime: I contacted the US immigration office to tell them that someone travelling on a passport under the name Alexander de Rothschild was almost certainly there on an expired visa, as he would only have been able to get a three-month tourist visa to enter the country.

It was a good feeling, knowing that he was oblivious to what was coming his way.

However, Philip and I telephoned DC Arkell the next day only to find our hope and excitement quashed.

She told us it would be difficult for her to do anything much as the police would need to apply for an international arrest warrant and an extradition order. This would take time, allowing Alexander to do a runner.

We were disconsolate – but not for long.

'What would happen if we went to the US and helped get him deported for overstaying his visa? Would that help?' Philip asked her.

I remember DC Arkell letting out a small giggle.

'You'd be handing him to us on a plate,' she told us.

It made sense – we didn't just want to leave it to officials, who we could not guarantee would operate as quickly as we would like. It would be good to have feet on the ground, as it were.

How could we do it, though? I wondered, as we got off the phone. We could barely afford a train ticket to London, never mind a flight to New York.

'Leave it to me, Chrissy. I am going to make this happen,' Philip told me, pulling me into a reassuring hug.

That night, Philip called his sister Lesley and asked if she could loan us the money to pay for our flights to the US. She readily agreed.

The following day, we flew out to New York. It was 11 April 2008, and although Alexander didn't know it, we were coming for him.

17

ACROSS THE POND

Our Virgin Atlantic flight touched down at Newark Airport at midnight and as we circled in the air, preparing to land, I wondered what on earth was in store for us. I was exhilarated but apprehensive about what lay ahead.

In the first instance, though, Philip and I had some practical obstacles to overcome. Kabira agreed to look after the children, but everything had happened in such a rush that we hadn't even managed to get any American dollars before we boarded our flight, something Philip had assured me I needn't worry about as we would surely be able to get some currency no matter what time we arrived in the city that never sleeps.

That turned out not to be the case: maybe they don't sleep in the bright lights of Manhattan, but Newark Airport was as dead as a rural English village in the small hours, and without any money – and at a time when taxi cabs didn't take debit cards – we were a bit stuck.

We'd booked a hotel in our final destination, Westchester County, but, too exhausted to do any onward travel, we had assumed we could just pitch up at a hotel near the airport for the first night. We'd tried a couple and had no luck and were wondering what to do when Helen, a Virgin ground crew member who had spotted us on the concourse looking slightly bewildered, came over and asked if we needed help.

We asked if she could recommend a hotel near the airport where we could bunk down for the remainder of the night, only for Helen to tell us that we were on a hiding to nothing: there was a big conference going on and not an available room for miles.

It seemed we were stymied before we had even started. I hoped this wasn't going to prove symbolic.

Luckily, Helen had the number for a local limousine company that would take payment in British pounds, although they couldn't come to pick us up for another two hours.

It was now nearing 2 a.m. and given that five hours later we were due to meet a local private investigator called Gil Alba at a hotel in Lincolndale, a town in Westchester County outside New York City, we had little option but to go straight there.

We arrived at 5 a.m., giving us a chance to snatch a fitful hour and a half's rest before we had to be up and out to make our rendezvous with Gil.

Tall and handsome with greying hair, Gil was a former New York cop who had already proved to be extremely thorough in our interaction so far.

We had talked at length on the phone the previous day and Gil had asked for a number of documents and newspaper articles to help check on my claims.

I sensed he was one of the good guys, and he put us at ease immediately, although after we'd exchanged pleasantries he told us we needed to get moving: while Philip and I had been winging our way across the Atlantic, he had already tracked Alexander down.

'I know exactly where he is right now, and it's at the gym about a fifteen-minute drive away,' he told me. 'If we go right now, we can confront him there.'

My heart leapt into my mouth: everything was moving so fast. I was exhausted after a long flight and having had very little sleep, and my tiredness was fuelled by a low-level anxiety. We were in unknown territory now, in a country where people carried guns. I had no idea how things were going to turn out.

Still, I had invested too much to turn back now.

'Let's go and ruin his day,' I said to Gil with a smile. I knew he would be horrified to see me.

Philip and I travelled with Gil in his car to the gym, where we were meeting a couple of his henchmen who had been keeping an eye on the place.

Also there to meet us was a photographer from the *Daily Mirror*. While Lesley had been kind enough to loan us the money for the flight, we still needed to cover our hotel bill and expenses, and getting the support of a national newspaper was the only way to do it that I could think of. This time it was the *Daily Mirror*. I had been dealing with one of the paper's journalists, Simon Wright, who had agreed that the paper would pay in return for an exclusive story.

The paper had a photographer called Dan Callister based in the city – he had taken the iconic photo of the dust-covered firefighters emerging from the Twin Towers on 9/11 – and I had called Simon just before we left the hotel to tell him where he needed to send Dan to capture a shot of the errant Mr de Rothschild.

In the event, Dan proved useful before he got his camera out. The big question was how to lure Alexander away from the gym floor without arousing suspicions, and it was Dan who came up with a good idea.

Gil knew Alexander's car registration, and I could barely suppress my astonishment when I realised that he was driving a blue Golf R32 – exactly the same make and model of car he had persuaded me to purchase a couple of years earlier.

Later we discovered that Julia Tyler had bought the car for $35,000 on a finance plan and Alexander had subsequently made a failed attempt to get the garage where she had purchased it to put the ownership out of her name and into his.

In the meantime, back in that gym car park, Dan suggested he go to reception and say he had clipped the Golf with his own car as he manoeuvred his way into a parking slot.

'That'll get him out,' he grinned.

Dan was absolutely right: a couple of minutes after he had gone in to spin his story to reception, Alexander came running out, clad in little pink gym shorts and with weights attached to his wrist.

It was surreal, seeing him in the flesh after all these months, and I was struck by what a ludicrous and pathetic figure he was, this predator who had ripped apart so many lives.

Tucked away behind another car, I watched as he bent down to survey the non-existent damage before walking up behind him.

'Hello, Alexander. Remember me?' I said, as I walked up behind him.

I'll never forget what happened next. Turning round to see me approaching, his face dropped, then he puffed out his chest and walked up to me, bumping his front into mine in some bizarre imitation of an alpha gorilla trying to see off a mating rival.

'Don't do this, Chrissy,' he said.

'Do what?' I replied, feigning surprise at his hostility. 'I've just come to bring you your bankruptcy documentation.'

At that point he turned on his heels and fled back into the gym.

'Don't worry, Alexander,' I shouted at his retreating form. 'I've put them under the wiper blades for you.'

I felt a rush of adrenalin. If nothing else I had found him – my determination to confront him prevailing, despite all the obstacles put in my way.

Nonetheless my moment of victory didn't last long, as Gil was keen to stay one step ahead of proceedings.

'We should get down to the police station, Chrissy,' he told me. 'We need to tell them what just happened in case he tries to make a complaint.'

It brought me back down to earth with a bump: the last thing I wanted was Alexander disappearing on me again. There was always that risk, of course, but I wanted him to know that I was onto him.

We headed immediately for the state police, although it proved to be a wasted trip.

The unfriendly red-headed officer we spoke to, whose name I can't recall, couldn't have been less interested in what we told him, particularly when I went on to outline the crimes he had committed in the UK.

'He hasn't committed a crime here,' he told me.

'What about the fact that his visa waiver has expired?' I pointed out. 'He's almost certainly overstayed by several months.'

The officer wasn't having this either. 'We have millions of people who overstay their visa in the US,' he told me.

I was surprised: I'd always been led to believe that the US of all countries was ferocious when it came to immigration transgressions, but apparently not.

Only after making it clear that we wouldn't leave without some further assistance did the officer snap. 'You can try the DA's office,' he told me. I'd watched enough American legal dramas to know this meant the District Attorney.

I was champing at the bit to go straight away, but Gil suggested we draw a line under it for the day. 'You've barely slept, Chrissy. I think give yourself a break and we can revisit stuff tomorrow,' he told me.

Reluctantly, I agreed. Philip and I were both running on adrenalin, and we still had to travel into Manhattan, where we were staying with Jane Goldberg, a psychotherapist who was also Bob Tyler's girlfriend. Hearing that we were coming over, Jane had kindly agreed to put us up in her flat in Manhattan.

Philip and I first went for lunch in Lincolndale, our sleep-deprived brains trying to process what had unfolded so far, before hailing a cab to the station to get the train into Manhattan.

I'll admit I was excited. I had never been to New York before, and while I hadn't anticipated the circumstances that would take me there, I was thrilled by the famous skyline and the city's frantic energy.

We arrived on West 22nd Street in Lower Manhattan to be met by Jane and Bob. Both in their fifties, they were lovely and did everything they could to put us at ease despite the odd circumstances of our meeting.

Jane cooked us dinner and we chatted at length about Alexander. As well as her personal interest as Bob's girlfriend, as a mental health expert she also had a professional interest.

'He sounds like a textbook sociopath to me,' she told me. 'A lack of conscience and empathy, a disregard for rules and norms, and impulsive and aggressive tendencies – they all tick the box.'

It was the first time I had heard the word, although I would come to hear and understand it a great deal more.

After a good night's sleep, Philip and I rose early the next day to travel back to Westchester County to visit the DA's office in a small town called White Plains – although first we had another stop to make.

The previous evening, Philip had pulled out his laptop and suggested I write a letter to Alexander setting out the situation as it stood – that he was bankrupt and would remain so until he complied with the UK Insolvency Service to provide a statement of his assets, and that the police in Cheltenham wanted to speak to him regarding my allegations against him of fraud, misrepresentation and theft.

'We want to make it look like he has a chance to make reparation now, otherwise he might just freak out and leave,' Philip pointed out.

He was right. Together we worked on a letter that was unemotional and factual, informing Alexander of my movements, giving him my mobile number once again and asking him to contact me to discuss repayment, otherwise I would give the police in Cheltenham his address in Lincolndale.

Of course, I was already in the process of making every legal authority possible aware of his whereabouts, but he didn't need to know that.

I ended it this way:

It is regretful that I have had to travel so far and waste so much time and money to force you to confront the serious financial situation you have left me in, together with my children. Even now, whether by talking to the police, contacting the Insolvency Service or making a realistic offer of repayment from your own resources, I hope you try to make amends.

'We'll deliver it to Julia's house tomorrow,' Philip said. I also sent an email to DS Paula Hannaford, who was then overseeing the separate investigation into Alexander's alleged abuse back in Stroud to tell her we had tracked him down.

I told her it was possible that someone from the DA's office might contact her to get her to back up the allegations I had made, and that I would be grateful if she could prioritise the call.

We woke the following day and made the journey to hand deliver my letter to Alexander at Julia Tyler's home. I was curious to see where he'd landed himself this time, and it was clear that he'd secured himself another desirable address in the form of a detached house in an affluent neighbourhood. Bob Tyler had already told me it was worth around $1.5 million, with a $400,000 mortgage I suspected Alexander would be busy trying to get his hands on.

We didn't ring the doorbell – my letter said everything I had to say – but we popped my missive through the letterbox before using public transport to get ourselves to the DA's office in the town of White Plains to register a formal complaint and also inform them that Alexander's visa must have expired.

It turned out to be another largely futile visit. The man we saw displayed the same disinterestedness as the officer we'd met in our previous encounter, although he did hear me out before telling me there was nothing he could do.

'You need to go to the US Marshals' office,' he told me.

I tried not to let my irritation show as we made our way across town to yet another legal department where, on arrival, we were directed down a small corridor to a small booth, where a young man no older than about twenty-five sat behind a glass screen.

It certainly didn't feel promising. The young man didn't say a word as I tried to set out why I was there in as brief an account as I could manage. Once I'd finished, there was a moment's silence before he told me to wait there.

Philip and I sat in the gloomy corridor as the minutes ticked by. What on earth was he doing? Whatever it was, it didn't feel particularly good, and my nerves were jangling when, around twenty minutes later, he came back and opened the window of his booth.

'You need to get yourself down to the FBI's office,' he told us. 'Special Agent Frank Gasper will be waiting for you.'

We were both stunned – the FBI? I hadn't even considered that they might be involved, although I wasn't going to argue. Gathering my files and my handbag, I motioned to Philip to go ahead of me and we hurriedly made our way out of the building and walked to the address we'd been given, which was also in White Plains.

Entering the local FBI building added another surreal layer to this trip. After passing through the multiple levels of security, Philip and I were escorted down corridors lined with pictures of the world's most-wanted men. Among them was Osama bin Laden.

We took the lift several floors up to another windowless room where Special Agent Frank Gasper was waiting to meet us.

We later got to know him reasonably well, but for now he was all business. Directing us to a couple of chairs, he said he had to contact Cheltenham Police Station to help verify our identities.

We listened as he made first that call and then a subsequent one to the FBI offices in London, which I hadn't even known existed until then, setting out the story we had told him so they could confirm who we were.

Then he turned to us and said, 'I'm all yours.'

Frank listened attentively as we went through our story for what felt like the umpteenth time. He was happy to take in the detail, which meant we were there for around an hour and a half as I furnished him with the timeline of my deception, Alexander's known crimes, what he was wanted for in the UK and my suspicions about what he was up to in the US.

He took detailed notes before suggesting we go out and get a bite to eat and then return after lunch.

When we came back, however, it didn't initially feel like good news. Frank Gasper said he had phoned the immigration offices but hadn't achieved much.

'The general vibe was, they would get round to looking into him at some point,' he told us.

I'll admit I was surprised, believing that a call from an FBI agent might warrant more immediate action. In fairness, Frank said the case was far from closed, and he suggested that the following day we took ourselves down to the Immigration and Customs Enforcement offices at City Hall in Manhattan to explain what was going on.

'If you tell them that you've got the British press with you and that you've spoken to the FBI, that should get them to pay attention,' he told us.

In the meantime, he offered to give us a lift to the station at White Plains so we could get the train back into Manhattan.

We returned to Jane's flat via a stiff drink at a local hotel bar, and had a good night's sleep before rising the next day and making our own way to the immigration offices: as I was in the city, I was determined to do everything I could to make sure every authority going was aware of Alexander's transgressions, and while they might indeed have millions overstaying their visa, not many of them would be a convicted fraudster wanted for the possible rape of an underage girl.

The Immigration and Customs Enforcement (ICE) offices were housed in a skyscraper, a towering vision with huge glass doors on the ground floor and populated by wall-to-wall gun-toting security guards.

The ICE's offices were housed on one of the upper floors and, after waiting a while, we were directed to a screen behind which sat an officious-looking lady who had 'jobsworth' written all over her face. Unhelpful doesn't even cover it: cold and off-hand, she kept handing me irrelevant forms and seemed determined not to listen to what I was trying to tell her.

Finally, she snapped.

'There is absolutely nothing I can do here,' she told me. 'When someone comes out of that door over there' – at this stage she motioned to a corner office – 'that will be an immigration officer. Speak to them.'

It seemed a little unorthodox, but we took her advice at face value and waited until someone emerged from the door she had gestured to, before intercepting him as he walked towards the lift.

'Can you give me a minute of your time?' I asked him. 'I have evidence that a serious criminal is overstaying his visa here.'

The guy looked at me, then after a moment's pause he told me to jump in the elevator with him. 'You need to make it quick as I'm on my lunch,' he told me.

It gave a new meaning to the term 'elevator pitch': as swiftly as I could I tried to summarise Alexander's situation and why I was there.

As the lift doors opened on the ground floor, the man – I never did learn his name – gave me the number of the Duty Officer and told me to call him and explain everything, which we did.

'Leave it with me,' said the Duty Officer, before abruptly ending the call.

Deflated, Philip and I walked out into the weak April sunshine and sat on a nearby bench. After the brief euphoria of my confrontation with Alexander, and the adrenalin surge from the involvement of the FBI, it felt like we were back at square one.

My biggest fear was that Alexander would do a runner. He knew we were there now, and while I had tried to sugar-coat my presence a little in my letter, there was every chance he sensed the net closing in and was planning his escape.

There didn't feel like there was much we could do about it, though. Slightly disheartened, we walked the streets of Manhattan for a while before having an early dinner of burgers and fries at a local diner and then heading back to Jane's.

We were due to fly home the following evening, and it seemed unlikely that there would be any resolution before we left.

'No one can say we didn't try,' I said to Philip, as I switched off the lamp next to our sofa bed.

I woke, startled, at 6 a.m. to the loud trill of the telephone on the side table next to where we were sleeping in the living room. Given that it wasn't my flat, it didn't feel right to answer it, but it rang so insistently that finally I felt I had no choice. Whoever was on the other end *really* wanted to make contact, it seemed.

Thank God I did pick up the handset, because Bob Tyler was on the other end of the line.

'Morning, Chrissy,' he said. 'I thought you'd like to know that the FBI and the INS [Immigration and Naturalization Service] went to Julia's house this morning and arrested Alexander in his bath towel.'

From what Bob said it had been every bit the dramatic dawn raid that you see in American crime dramas: armed officers had surrounded the house in case Alexander had tried to escape their clutches.

My jaw dropped as I took in the news. I can honestly say it was one of the best phone calls I've ever received.

'I don't know much more at this stage,' Bob went on. 'I do know Julia was protesting, telling the police they were going to get married and they had made a mistake. It's kinda sad.'

I couldn't help but agree. It was impossible not to feel sorry for her, as I knew Alexander had reeled her in every bit as effectively as he had me.

Mainly, though, what I felt as I replaced the receiver was pure euphoria. I didn't know what would happen to Alexander now, but one way or another he would face justice – and I had made it happen.

A couple of hours later, Philip and I were strolling by Pier 17 in Lower Manhattan, a popular open-air venue within the city's seaport. We were only there as Philip had suggested we spend the day sightseeing ahead of our flight home that night, and we hadn't been there long when my mobile phone rang.

It was a New York number that I didn't recognise, but given the news we'd received only a short while ago, it seemed worth answering.

It was Julia Tyler on the end of the line.

'Hi, Chrissy, it's Julia,' she said, her voice cool, though not hostile. 'I think we need to chat.'

She suggested we meet at the office where she worked as a nutritionist, which was located uptown.

I was happy to go; if nothing else, I felt she deserved to know the truth about the man with whom she apparently believed herself in love. I could only imagine what a shock it must have been having the FBI turn up on her doorstep that morning.

Philip and I agreed that it would be best if I went alone, and around half an hour later I arrived in the lobby of her office block, located in yet another huge high-rise building on one of Manhattan's main north–south thoroughfares.

Grey-haired and attractive, Julia was smartly dressed in a suit and was friendly enough as she beckoned me into her small office, extending her hand to shake mine.

I'm not sure what I'd been expecting, but there was none of the angst or bewilderment that you might expect from someone whose partner has just been arrested in a very dramatic way and whose life has just fallen apart. Indeed, as we chatted it became abundantly clear that she had been entirely sucked in by Alexander's lies.

'I guess I need to hear your side of the story, because what Alexander has told me isn't remotely flattering,' she said.

Julia went on to say that Alexander had spoken of me at some length in the past, telling her I was an ongoing thorn in his side – a woman scorned who had willingly given him money, then become resentful when he refused to marry her.

I'd apparently then started a campaign of harassment against both him and his family, who she had also been in touch with. 'I've spoken to them a number of times and they have been very welcoming,' she told me.

It wasn't easy listening to this, but I tried to detach myself emotionally. As I saw it, I was there as a messenger, to tell Julia why I had come to New York and to fill her in on her lover's extensive criminal background.

I'd been in her shoes, and I knew it would take her time to digest what had happened, so it didn't surprise me in the slightest when she told me she was sorry to hear about what I'd told her, but it was different for her as she wasn't financially involved with him.

It was fairly obvious she didn't fully believe me, and although it didn't really matter to me what she thought, and despite my determination to remain detached, we both cried.

I hadn't shed a single tear since I'd arrived in New York, but suddenly there, in that small office, trying to explain to a woman who, to all intents and purposes, was me four years earlier just brought it all home.

In fairness, Julia was sympathetic, clutching my hand, and after I'd been to the bathroom to freshen up she was much warmer towards me, although she still didn't give much away.

We parted on terms as decent as we could considering the circumstances in which we'd met, although it would take Julia some time to see Alexander for who he truly was, which I could understand. I'd been there.

Gil Alba found it harder to understand. He had even gone to see her of his own volition to tell her that she needed to confront the truth, only to find her prevaricating about what she wanted to believe.

'She is still not convinced, but for her sake she is going to have to weigh all of her own choices,' he wrote to me in an email dated 19 April, shortly after I had returned to the UK. 'I told her that in a month she will be calling you and thanking you.' I had done what I had come to New York to do, and it was now in the hands of both the US and British authorities. I knew from Gil that Alexander was fighting deportation, although the fact that he had entered the US on a visa waiver meant he had no entitlement to a hearing. Julia Tyler had apparently gone to visit him and again told officials that they were due to get married – giving him the opportunity to apply for the coveted Green Card which would get him permanent residency in the States – although as Gil said it was a bit late for that. The only recourse he could possibly have would be to claim asylum, but it would be an odd government who granted asylum to a man on rape charges.

In any case, whatever was happening to Alexander, I just wanted to get home. It had been an exhilarating but exhausting few days, and all I could think of was walking through my front door and giving my children an enormous hug.

A few hours after I parted company with Julia Tyler, Philip and I boarded another Virgin flight, this time heading for London, and for what would turn out to be several turbulent months ahead.

18

FIGHTING ON

Philip and I arrived back in England exhausted, although I was excited by the prospect of seeing my children, who I'd missed hugely and who jumped into my arms as if I'd been away for a year when I went to pick them up from school.

I didn't have long to catch my breath. Within hours of getting home, my landline started to ring and when I answered I found Julia Tyler on the other end of the line.

She had been to see Alexander at the deportation centre shortly after I had left, and – naturally – he had accused me again of spreading all manner of vile lies.

'I just don't know what to make of it all, Chrissy,' she said to me in the first of what would prove to be a series of phone calls and lengthy emails in which she went back and forth between my version of events and Alexander's.

I did sympathise with her – I had been in her shoes, inhabiting that weird alternate reality that Alexander had been so good at creating. At the same time, it was hard not to feel frustrated, not least because it was difficult to be confronted with her oscillating emotions at a time when I was struggling to manage my own.

I also returned home to find an email from Carla Perkins – the ex-lover of Alexander who had previously contacted me as 'Sabrina' – waiting for me on my computer.

I had dropped her a line before I left for New York, telling her what had happened in case it prompted her into further correspondence, and it seemed to have done the trick.

It wasn't a long email, but it did shed further light on their interactions. The two had connected on Match.com in 2006 and corresponded for several months. They met in person in January 2007 shortly after she had come out of hospital after a serious illness and – as was his modus operandi – he had quickly promised her the moon on a stick. His 'cover' was that he was a legitimate Rothschild with a robust fortune to his name, which he wanted to share with her. He had told her that he would buy a large house into which she and her three children would move and that she could focus on making her name as an artist – but in return she suspected that he wanted her to sell her apartment in Florida's Fort Lauderdale, just as he had persuaded me to sell my home, and then access the money.

She had been curious enough about his grandiose claims to google him, though, at which point she had come across one of my newspaper interviews. Confronting him, she had been told in response that I was – this old chestnut again – a liar who was bitterly stalking him because he had ended our relationship.

'He was extremely convincing,' she wrote. 'He seems to have quite a story and an explanation for just about everything, including government secrecy. I really did not know what to believe.'

Nonetheless, as a single mother of three she had taken the decision to walk away and move on with her life. Now, she wondered if he had just been using her for marriage, and the American citizenship and credit that could follow.

'I believe he even tried to get my personal information to steal my identity,' she added, ending by saying she believed that he had been in New York for some time but had also been seeing a woman in North Carolina.

It all sounded like textbook Alexander: in his email to me, Julia's nephew had said he had gathered that Alexander was frequently away from his aunt's home for days at a time – giving assorted excuses as to why – and it was now becoming clear that even while he was living with Julia in Lincolndale he had been spinning many other female plates elsewhere.

It was bewildering even thinking about the extent of the web of lies he had spun, although in those early days after arriving home from the US I was preoccupied with something far more pressing, which was finding out exactly what had happened to Alexander now he had been taken into custody.

For that I had to rely on Frank Gaspar. On 25 April, just over a week after Philip and I had returned home, he called me to say that Alexander had been put on a flight to the UK, escorted by two US agents.

The plane touched down at Gatwick Airport at 7.20 a.m. the following morning, at which point Alexander was immediately placed under arrest on suspicion of molestation and fraud.

Later, I learned that as the uniformed police officers approached him he had said, 'I know what this is about – this is about my son's mother.' It seemed that even in one of his lowest moments he was trying to make it sound like it was a personal vendetta on my part, rather than his own criminality.

Alexander was taken to Cheltenham Police Station where he was questioned and held overnight before appearing at Cheltenham Magistrates' Court the following day, where he was charged with several fraud-related offences. It was a bittersweet moment – on the one hand I was thrilled, but I was also harbouring a deep anxiety that Alexander might be granted bail. If he was, then there was no question in my mind that he would disappear in an instant, and everything I had worked to achieve so far would evaporate into thin air.

I was cheered by the fact that John Price had supplied a detailed statement to Cheltenham Police setting out his own interactions with Alexander and emphasising that he was a serious flight risk. Surely the courts would take his previous convictions and behaviour into account when they made their decision?

Nonetheless, I was on tenterhooks as I waited for the crucial call from DC Arkell, who was still overseeing the fraud investigation in Cheltenham in parallel with the ongoing sexual assault investigation in Stroud, and when she told me he had been refused bail pending his trial, I realised that I had effectively been holding my breath for three days straight. This time, at least, the authorities had got things right.

DC Arkell told me that Alexander had been remanded to

Gloucester Prison, where, by coincidence, a fellow parent at the children's school worked.

'He's not very popular in there,' he told me at the school gates a few days later. 'He's trying to play the big "I am" but everyone can see straight through him.'

I had to smile. It seemed that even the humble confines of a prison cell could not restrict Alexander's ego – although at least in there he couldn't do anyone any harm.

Emotionally I was struggling. My initial euphoria at helping to get Alexander back to the UK and starting the process I fervently hoped would end with him facing justice quickly faded and was replaced with the dull ache of reality.

While it was morale-boosting to think he might now be punished for his deeds, there was no changing the devastation he had left behind in my life, not just financially but on every level imaginable.

Not long after I'd returned from the US, I had shown Marcus a picture of his father, and for the first time he hadn't recognised him. It was a moment of conflict, leaving me both relieved and sad. Relieved that he didn't appear to miss him, but sad that this innocent boy had been made a victim by a man for whom it seemed any human being, whatever their age, was just collateral damage.

I also worried for my other children. While I had tried to shelter them as much as I could from the unfolding dramas, and while the presence of Clive in their lives gave them some emotional and financial stability – and Philip, who they genuinely liked, also gave a lot of support – they were only too aware of our change in circumstances, and I knew they no longer looked on the world as the benign place it had once been for them. As the youngest, Sarah in particular seemed bewildered, repeatedly asking questions about the future.

I'd also had to go to the children's school to talk to the teachers about the fact that there might be some press attention, as Alexander's arrest and the fact that he had been charged had made the newspapers.

'I am trying to prepare them as best I can for what lies ahead but it may be that other children start asking them questions,' I told one staff member. 'I just want you to be aware, as there may be some rocky roads ahead.'

Meanwhile there was no escaping the fact that my own financial situation was pretty desperate.

My one hope was that while Alexander had taken a huge amount of money from me, I believed he couldn't have spent it all. I assumed there were some investments, alongside the existence of a large number of his personal possessions, which were bound to have some value, given Alexander's affection for designer labels.

There was money out there, I told Philip. Our job now was trying to track down exactly where it was and how we could get it back.

For that, we needed to liaise with Julia, as we knew that Alexander had left a large amount of goods at her house, which technically now belonged to the Insolvency Service.

Sadly, Julia was still struggling to confront the truth. In what felt like a flood of emails over the course of April and

May, she poured out her heart about how she struggled to accept that Alexander was capable of everything I had described to her. Even the newspaper articles I had sent her were not enough to convince her.

As the weeks went by it was also clear that she was being put under pressure to ship Alexander's possessions back to the UK.

'You can't do that, Julia,' I told her in one call. 'Any possessions of his now belong to the Insolvency Service so you would be breaking the law.'

All I could do was try to continually reassure her that it was now time for the appropriate authorities to deal with Alexander.

Now that the scales had completely dropped from my eyes it was difficult trying to handhold someone else who was at the start of the process. Julia seemed to want to endlessly debate Alexander's background, and it also became clear that she was trying to find excuses for his behaviour.

All we knew for sure was that he had caused immense harm to others. I had to remind myself that, ultimately, I couldn't be responsible for Julia's decisions and her take on what had happened. All I could do was tell her the truth and let her come to her own conclusions.

Still, it was getting trickier and trickier not to lose my cool with her, particularly as she was putting obstacles in my way on a practical level. I had asked her repeatedly to release Alexander's goods to the insolvency practitioner – after which I could in theory reclaim some of their value – but she replied that she was 'not in a position to do anything that is not a formal request that would be valid in this jurisdiction'. When, by June, Philip had made yet another failed attempt to ask Julia to assist in the return of Alexander's assets, we had to take the decision to retain the services of a bankruptcy attorney in White Plains – more expense – in order to issue something called a 'Chapter 15 notice', obliging Julia to assist us in pursuing assets belonging to Alexander and held by her that were of interest to the insolvency practitioner.

Back in the UK we also had to get further paperwork, including something called a Deed of Assignment, issued by the insolvency practitioner, which would give us the authority to go to New York and collect the goods.

All this would ultimately take months, and in the meantime Alexander was still trying his old emotional tricks. On 9 June, I received another email from Julia's son Nate saying that his mum had been getting calls from Alexander claiming that all charges against him were to be dropped. 'Is that true?' he asked.

All I could do was reassure him that the legal wheels were turning over here, and it looked as if everything was moving towards a trial.

'I'm really sorry to hear that your mum is still being sucked into this. I feel for her,' I replied. 'She is probably under a lot of pressure. Alexander and his family can be very difficult.'

Life at home was not without its intrigue either. Determined to try to get as much information as possible to backfill Alexander's movements in the time we had been together, Philip suggested that we invite Tracey over for dinner.

'After a glass of wine or two it will be interesting to see if she lets anything slip,' he told me.

I could see his logic, but I wasn't keen. Tracey was no friend of mine. As it was, Philip prevailed and on the evening of 17 May Tracey came to supper with her new boyfriend, Daniel.

During that first dinner – something we followed up with a couple of other dinners during the course of the year, largely because Philip liked Daniel so much – Tracey made a comment that surprised me.

At one point we were discussing my pregnancy with Marcus – the pregnancy which she would later tell the police in her witness statement had caused her to leave Alexander and move out of the house.

'You didn't have an easy time, did you?' she asked. 'I remember that day you sent Alexander an email telling him you were having a bleed.'

It was hard to conceal my sharp intake of breath. If she had walked away from him romantically during my pregnancy, would he have been sharing such intimate details? The bleed had happened around the twelve-week mark, while Tracey had insisted that she had left him in April, a couple of months previously, and not returned until much later in the year after being worn down by him. Of course, it was possible that they had remained in touch, but it seemed odd that he would be sharing this kind of intimate detail if so. Either way, Tracey determinedly stuck to her story that while she knew Alexander had come into money because of the changes he had made to his lifestyle, she believed him when he said that I was a benefactor until news of my pregnancy emerged.

In the meantime the sexual assault case against Alexander was now working its way through the legal system and I received an official call concerning the trial from DC Sharon Matthews from Stroud Police.

'We wondered if you could give a statement about your relationship with Alexander and the victim [who I had met through Alexander]?' she asked.

I replied that that would be fine, although I also made it clear that I didn't feel I had a great deal to add, as I hadn't known anything about what was going on.

'I did think their relationship was odd, but there were a lot of odd things about Alexander, so I didn't make too much of it,' I told her.

DC Matthews told me that whatever I had to say was fine – my statement was all part of the ongoing building of the case. Nonetheless, setting down my thoughts was difficult, as it made everything more real. The man I had once loved was being charged with four counts of rape and three counts of sexual abuse of a minor.

The bureaucracy left in Alexander's wake was sometimes overwhelming, especially dealing with the endless correspondence to do with the ongoing bankruptcy. As a result of Alexander's bankruptcy, however, I was able to apply for access to his bank accounts. While it took many months to get my hands on the statements, they made very interesting reading when they finally dropped onto the doormat around September 2009.

The first discovery that led my jaw to drop was seeing the vast sums that had gone in and out of Alexander's account –

tens of thousands at a time; all from me, of course. The second discovery was that he had been receiving Jobseekers' Allowance. He also had large overdrafts from the bank, and one account had the wrong address on it.

As I later complained to the bank, how could they not have questioned the transactions, given the vast sums involved and their conjunction with a state allowance for someone on the breadline? Their response was that the allowance could have been paid on behalf of someone else without access to a bank account – but as I pointed out, the reference was his name and National Insurance number.

In the meantime, despite everything that was going on, I was also trying to keep my family afloat. No matter how hard Philip and I tried to raise money, we were losing it hand over fist.

The financial crash that had begun in 2007 had continued to hit everyone's pockets, and Philip's book stall sales had plummeted. Paying the rent had become a hopeless proposition, and the time-consuming process of trying to bring Alexander to justice meant there was still no time for me to get a job. I was relying increasingly on bits of income from selling any goods I owned of even the vaguest value, from jewellery to furniture to the sale of the few goods from Alexander's storage unit which I had purchased from the auctioneer.

At one point I managed to sell a model yacht he owned for £150, which allowed me to buy Christmas presents for the children in the last hour of 24 December, when some shops start their sale.

There's no question that everything that was going on was taking its toll on me. Sometimes it was a fight to get through each day. I still wasn't sleeping, and I'd also started having heart palpitations and nosebleeds. On one occasion, I was standing at the counter of a local corner shop buying milk when my nose started gushing with blood and I had to rush outside, leaving my carton of milk on the counter. I was a mess, but I knew I didn't have any choice but to keep going.

19

BACK TO NEW YORK ...
AND AN UNUSUAL SALE

With the dawn of New Year 2009, I was filled with a renewed determination to get Alexander's stuff back from America. We had all the legal paperwork in place from the insolvency practitioner, giving us permission to retrieve the goods on his behalf, and together Philip and I had been putting the pressure on Julia in recent weeks, aided by Bob, who was trying to get his ex-wife to see sense too.

The insolvency practitioner had also agreed that we could sell any goods we retrieved privately as we were likely to command a higher price than at auction. That money would then go back to the practitioner to be put into the pot to pay back Alexander's creditors – which in the main was me.

The threat of issuing a Chapter 15 notice – something we had held off doing so far, although we had continued to retain the services of the White Plains attorney just in case – did seem to have focused her mind, although she was still prevaricating.

Then, late in the afternoon on Monday, 23 February, Bob rang to say Julia would cooperate if we had the right legal paperwork.

'She said if you book flights in a few days then that works – but you need to have those documents with you,' he told us.

I sighed inwardly. We'd been asking the insolvency practitioner about the deed of assignment that authorised us to take Alexander's possessions back to the UK for months, but like everything else, that had a bureaucratic edge and getting the right paperwork in place was a process that seemed to move at a glacial place.

By now, though, I was just getting so sick of waiting that I took the decision to book a flight anyway, putting them on one of the few credit cards I now had that wasn't maxed out.

Once more, Kabira was left to hold the fort with the children.

'It's just a few days again,' I told them as I cuddled them at bedtime the night before my flight.

The following day Philip and I arrived at the airport in a tense mood, as the insolvency practitioner had still not issued the Deed of Assignment.

'Do you know what, Philip?' I said as we queued to check in. 'We just have to get on the flight and work it out at the other end.'

It would take two whole days for the practitioner to get his act together, eventually faxing the documents we needed to a shop close to our hotel in Lincolndale, where we had first arrived nearly a year ago when I had confronted Alexander in the car park of his gym.

The moment the documents arrived we called Gil Alba, whose presence we knew would ensure we could not be accused of doing anything that wasn't to the legal letter. He in turn phoned Julia to say we were on our way.

We arrived at Julia's home on a glorious but chilly New York morning of blue skies and a piercing wind. I noticed that she'd dressed up for the occasion with a full face of make-up and a baby doll dress – perhaps her way of putting on a suit of armour in the face of what was undoubtedly a humiliating situation.

She was friendly enough, at first at least, beckoning us into a home which felt like an interior-designed set right down to the elevator music playing softly in the background.

Gesturing us into her large sitting room, she introduced us to a man she described as her friend, although in fact she would later go on to marry him.

We exchanged pleasantries before Julia asked if we wanted to see Alexander's stuff, beckoning us through her hall into the dining room.

Awaiting us was a scene not remotely like the one I'd antic-ipated: Philip and I had assumed that everything would be boxed up or in suitcases, but instead we were met by a scene I can only describe as chaotic.

In front of us was a mêlée of clothes, shoes and boxes dumped on a large dining-room table and strewn over the floor, alongside paperwork and empty bags.

The room was rammed, and I tried to keep my emotions in check as I surveyed the Louis Vuitton luggage and the boxes from Tiffany and Prada.

This had all been bought with *my* money. Alexander had made me penniless so he could parade around town in designer gear, duping other women into doing the same.

Julia quickly pulled me out of my reverie.

'What can I say? There's a lot of stuff,' she said with a shrug. 'I'll leave you to it.'

I remember looking at Philip, wondering how on earth we would deal with it.

'Let's get stuck in,' he said.

We started trying to pull things out methodically, sorting through every item one by one, but it quickly became clear that this was going to take hours, and as Julia kept on popping in to see how we were getting on – although in reality clearly wanting us out of her home – it all started to feel a bit awkward.

Eventually Philip turned to me and told me we just needed to get out. 'Let's ram it into bags and sort through it back at the hotel,' he said.

There was so much stuff that we had to phone for a people carrier to come to the house, and after loading it the brim and signing the paperwork with Julia, witnessed by her friend, we said our goodbyes.

Both Philip and I were a bit overwhelmed. Assuming the trip would be a quick in and out, we were booked on a flight to leave that night and it seemed inconceivable that we could sort out everything we needed to before then, not least because we weren't sure how we would deal with the US customs side of things. There was no way we could organise for goods to be shipped out of the country without knowing exactly what they were.

It was Philip who came up with a plan. He suggested we find a storage unit, shove everything in there and then return to sort through it when we had more time on our side. It was far from ideal, not least because of the expense, but we had no other options, as we couldn't change our flight home.

After asking at our hotel, we located a UPS unit nearby where, after another expensive taxi ride, we deposited our goods, locked the door and walked away before heading to the airport a couple of hours later.

Back in the UK, we spent the week flitting between the usual domestic jobs and the school run, while also taking legal advice on what to do with the stuff from New York and telephoning shipping companies.

None of it was boding well – we were continually asked exactly what we would be shipping and, although most of it seemed to be clothes and accessories, the reality was that we hadn't had time to go through it properly, so we didn't exactly know. I had visions of some dramatic customs interrogation over a random bit of electrical equipment or a designer item that I hadn't accounted for.

In the end, after yet another round of fruitless telephone calls to shipping companies, I made a snap decision.

'I think it's easiest if I just fly out on my own, pack everything into the suitcases and bring it back on the flight, paying for the excess luggage,' I told Philip. 'Anything I think might cause an issue I will leave behind.'

Thank goodness for Helen, our contact at Virgin. When I called her and explained the situation, she said she would help however she could. And so, two weeks after I'd returned to the UK, I travelled to New York again, this time on my own.

After flying into Newark, I spent the night in Manhattan with Jane Goldberg before travelling the following day to Lincolndale and retrieving all the goods from the unit.

Back in my hotel room I started to go through the bags methodically one by one. It wasn't easy: much as I tried to maintain an emotional distance from what I was doing, it was hard not to feel sickened as I sorted through item after item. There was everything from Montblanc pens to Tiffany cufflinks and collar stiffeners, Ralph Lauren shirts and Prada elephant-skin slippers – my money, my life, transposed into *this*. I despised him then, not just for his greed, but for his vanity.

As I packed them all carefully back into the designer luggage he'd left behind – Mulberry holdalls and Louis Vuitton suitcases that were worth thousands in themselves – I also stumbled across another item of interest. Inside a leather ledger was a collection of receipts and flight manifests, showing that Philomena's card was used to pay for Alexander's flights to the US from Geneva, and his onward flight from New York to Palm Beach, though knowing Alexander he may have used it himself.

Working through Alexander's goods took me a whole day, and when I arrived at Newark Airport on Sunday evening for my flight home I had so much luggage that I needed a special trolley to carry it. I couldn't help smiling at the thought that I must look like a celebrity off on tour with my teetering pile of designer luggage.

Less amusing was the excess luggage cost, which was around £500, and that was with Helen giving me a discount. I couldn't help but reflect on the irony that while, as with all my other expenses, I had to put this on a credit card to get it back to the UK, I could barely afford to buy a cup of coffee and a sandwich, and was grateful beyond belief when Helen gave me access to the VIP lounge where I could eat and drink for free.

Arriving back at Heathrow the following morning, I was met by Philip who had driven to collect me in his trusty Mondeo. We only just got everything in – by the time we had crammed the last bag into the back we couldn't see out of the windows and I had to sit for the two-hour journey home with a suitcase on my lap.

More paperwork followed at home as it was agreed with the insolvency practitioner that we could sell the goods privately as long as we gave him a percentage of what we made.

What I couldn't quite work out was how exactly to sell it. Ebay was an obvious option, but I wasn't sure I could handle the endless administration and toing and froing from the post office. I was still mulling it over during an appointment with my hairdresser, Paco (who in the good old days I had gone to every few weeks but now I only visited once a year), when he came up with an unexpected solution.

'I've got an empty room upstairs, Chrissy,' he said. 'Why don't you turn it into a pop-up boutique?'

The more I thought about it, the more I liked the idea. It was a one-stop shop if you like – quite literally – and took away the need to deal with postage.

A date was set for the end of May, and by the time we opened the doors at 7 p.m. I had to say that I'd done a good job, ably assisted by Paco and Philip. We had tables and shelves, all loaded with nicely arranged designer paraphernalia. Soft music played in the background, and we'd lit the room nicely to add to the boutique feel.

I'd relied on word of mouth, so I had no idea how busy it would be, and I was pleasantly surprised when a steady stream of customers came through the door.

What's more, by the end of the evening we had sold every last item, right down to Alexander's Ralph Lauren boxer shorts. When we counted up at the end of the evening, we had raised £12,000.

It was bittersweet: on the one hand it was a fraction of the estimated £80,000 the goods were collectively worth and a drop in the ocean of what Alexander had taken from me, but it was enough to help me settle my outstanding legal bills and gave me a bit of breathing space. I marked it up as a small victory.

May had seen another significant milestone in my quest for justice, as Alexander finally stood trial in relation to his crimes involving the sexual abuse of a minor.

The case had been scheduled to start three months earlier, but in actions that would foreshadow what would happen at his fraud trial, Alexander pulled every trick in the book to delay things, citing that his human rights were being abused, that he was the victim of racism and that he couldn't properly work on his defence. One excuse followed another until he had simply run out of options, and finally his trial opened at the start of May at Bristol Crown Court.

My main preoccupation in the lead-up had been how I would feel setting eyes on Alexander again for the first time since I had handed over his bankruptcy papers in that gym car park in Lincolndale.

I told myself I had to remain neutral, that I was there to do one job. And so I remained as calm as I could as I was ushered into the witness box by a court official, glancing over at Alexander in the dock to let him know I wasn't intimidated by him.

I received back nothing but a blank stare, although I couldn't help noticing that he looked decidedly more unkempt and dishevelled than before.

As clearly as I could, and gently encouraged by the prosecution barrister, I set out the points I had made in my witness statement, and then I was free to go. I stepped down from the witness box, left the court and got the train home. I'm not ashamed to admit I had a little cry when I let myself in through the front door. I prided myself on being strong, but sometimes the reality of what had happened to me and the monster I had let into my life hit me square in the face, and this was one of those times.

Three days later, I received a telephone call from Stroud Police informing me that Alexander had been found unanimously guilty on all charges – four counts of rape and three counts of sexual assault – but sentencing had been put on hold pending my own trial.

In some way this was a relief, as it meant the story would not be in the public eye for a while. I told myself it was my turn next.

June started with a lovely surprise: waking up one morning, I found Philip brandishing a cup of coffee and an airline ticket.

'You're off to Spain for a week,' he grinned.

I couldn't believe it. We couldn't afford a wet weekend in Scunthorpe, never mind the Spanish costas.

Philip explained that I was going to stay with John Price and his wife, Eva. John and Philip had cooked up the surprise between them. Philip had been worried about my health and state of mind for some time, while John had become a good friend to us both. They'd decided to try to give me a boost by giving me a week away at John's home in Andalucía.

I was insanely touched. A week in the sun away from it all, reading books and soaking up the rays, was the best medicine I could have hoped for.

By day I lounged on John and Eva's roof terrace, and at night we sat nursing a lovely glass of local red wine and putting the world to rights. I came home feeling, if not quite like a new woman, then certainly a rejuvenated one.

On my return, my main concern was getting through my own trial. Alexander had spent much of 2009 attempting to delay proceedings, and by the time it finally unfolded at Bristol Crown Court the police told me he had been through ten different defence teams. As I was to discover, further madness was to come.

20

THE COURT CASE

I've always had a degree of personal horror at the idea of going to court in any capacity, dating back to when my father did jury service when I was a child. By all accounts the case in which he was asked to produce a verdict was fairly grim, and I must have picked up on something as it left me with a residual fear of being called to do jury service myself, or indeed having anything to do with the court process.

My county court activities hadn't bothered me much – they felt more like bureaucratic procedures – but I'd been nervous in the days running up to being a witness in the trial relating to sexual offences against a minor.

Now, Alexander's looming court case left me with a mass of conflicting emotions: this was a case I was at the centre of, and it would doubtless unfold in front of a court packed with press and a curious public in the gallery. So, while I desperately wanted it to go ahead, I was highly anxious.

None of this had been helped by Alexander's endless manoeuvrings. He really had tried everything – one of his final strategies had been to suggest that press interest had meant he was subject to excess searches in his jail cell, and he had also asked for a permanent stay to proceedings on the basis that he had no chance of a fair trial, which thankfully was declined.

He must finally have run out of delaying tactics as I received a message from one of the administrative staff at Bristol Crown Court that the trial was starting on Monday, 22 February 2010.

Prior to that, they offered me the chance to visit the courtroom where the trial would take place to get a sense of how it would all work. I was grateful for that, as it meant that I knew what to expect when I turned up.

In fact, while the case did open on the Monday, it was delayed again until Friday of that week to give yet another of Alexander's newly assigned legal teams further time to prepare. As the chief witness for the prosecution case, I was told I would likely be called to give evidence on the following Monday.

I'd been told that the Crown Prosecution Service (CPS) would pay my costs to travel to the court, but I declined. Alexander had been such a drain on the public purse that it was a matter of honour to me to pay my own way. And so, on the morning of Monday, 1 March, I bought a ticket from Cheltenham to Bristol Temple Meads and, on arrival, jumped into a cab to the court.

I was travelling alone. Philip had offered to accompany me, but this was something I felt I had to face by myself. Even so, I couldn't help wishing I'd asked him to come with me when, pulling up at the bottom of the street that leads to the courthouse, I could see that a crowd had gathered outside, some of them with cameras.

'There must be something big going on today,' the cab driver remarked. 'There's lots of press here.'

'I think that might be something to do with me,' I said wryly as I disembarked.

I walked down the street to the court to the pop of flash-bulbs. It was hard not to feel self-conscious, although I'd dressed smartly for the occasion in a grey tweed shift dress, long grey wool coat and boots.

After clearing security at the court, I was sent to the witness suite where I waited with a knot of butterflies in my stomach. I felt incredibly anxious. During Alexander's sexual assault trial I'd been able to keep a degree of emotional distance, but this was different. I knew that it all hinged on me.

Finally, after around half an hour or so, a court usher came in and said they were asking for me. My stomach dropped: this was it.

The walk to court felt like the longest one I had ever taken, and as I walked through the doors into what was a packed courtroom and made my way towards the witness box, I took a deep breath and thought, 'Here goes, Chrissy.'

Just as you see on television dramas, I swore on the Bible to tell the truth and nothing but the truth.

From where I was standing – I declined to sit – the prose-cution and defence teams were in front of me, the jury straight ahead and the judge to my right, while Alexander was in the dock at the far end of the room to my left.

From the corner of my eye I could just about see the public gallery, where I had been told Philomena and Fred were sitting. Lydia and Theresa were also in the building, although they never came into the courtroom.

Once more, I deliberately made eye contact once – and once only – with Alexander, who, I noted, looked even more dishevelled than he did last time I'd set eyes on him.

Finally, the prosecution barrister, Michael Mather-Lees, stood up to begin his questions. By then, the jury had already heard an outline of what they could expect to hear from me in his opening statement – that I had been systematically targeted and fed a pack of lies by Alexander about his background and his endeavours.

'He acted without any scruples, as a conman,' he had told them.

Standing there, about to have my life laid open in front of a room full of strangers, I knew I had to disengage from my emotions and deal in the facts. The jury didn't need hysteria, they needed the truth as I remembered it, and it was my job to give it to them.

I was in the witness box all day, and while it was a physically and emotionally gruelling experience, I stepped down at the end of the afternoon feeling like a weight had been lifted from my shoulders. I knew the hardest bit was to come as I would be cross-examined the following day, but I had said what I needed to say.

Alexander was still up to his old tricks, though. After returning to the witness suite, I met DC Arkell, who told me that we had an issue. While giving evidence, I'd mentioned my diaries, and the defence team now wanted to see them for themselves.

The request made my blood boil. My diaries were largely a factual record of events and appointments and on the whole made for very dull reading, but they were still personal. It was also hard to shake the feeling that this was being driven by Alexander, another act of manipulation.

'No way,' I replied.

DC Arkell screwed up her face.

'Saying no doesn't look good, Chrissy, as it looks like you have something to hide,' she said.

I hated to have to admit it, but she was right, and so, taking a breath, I replied that it was OK.

'I'm not the one covering anything up here, DC Arkell,' I told her.

'This is typical Alexander,' I told Philip later as, now safely ensconced back in Eldorado Road, I gathered my diaries together.

It was then that Philip had an idea, pointing out that the only bits of the diary that were relevant to the case were from the day I met Alexander to the time he disappeared.

'Let's section off the pages before and after with tape,' he said.

I had to smile. I suspected the defence would insist on unfettered access, but it would be good to make a point. It was just my small way of pushing back.

Twelve hours later, on Tuesday morning, I retraced my steps and once more made my way from my home to Bristol Crown Court, where I handed over my diaries to DC Arkell.

As I predicted, the defence immediately said they needed to open the taped-off bits. I'll confess, it made me giggle. If they wanted to wade through a litany of children's dental and doctor's appointments and school plays, then they were welcome to do so.

My moment of amusement didn't last long. I knew that today's activity in the witness box would be tough, and that my evidence would be continually contested.

I wasn't wrong. From the outset, Charlotte Holland, one of two barristers representing Alexander, systematically tried to tear apart my evidence, painting me as a mentally unhinged gold-digger.

'You wanted to trap him – marry him because he was a member of the Rothschild family,' she asked, barely ten minutes after I had first entered the witness box.

'Not at all,' I replied.

On and on it went. There was nothing that Ms Holland didn't try to challenge. I knew that I couldn't rise to it and that I had to remain calm and collected in the face of what, on occasions, felt like huge provocation.

Of course, that's what defence teams try to do: prod and probe to get you to trip yourself up or lose your temper and say something that doesn't help your case.

The one time I did nearly lose my cool, however, was when Alexander's barrister suggested that social services had been in touch over concern about my children.

This was entirely false, and Alexander knew it – but he was canny enough to know that even a mention in court might put suspicion about my conduct in the jury's mind, which is why I assume he had given this 'information' to his legal team.

It was disgusting, and the one time when I couldn't control my emotions: placing my hands on the front of the witness box, I leaned forward and angrily said, 'That is an out and out lie.'

On another occasion, Ms Holland challenged me on a small joke I had made in my evidence the previous day, when I had mentioned that Alexander would often ask for a massage on his return from his fictional lengthy days hunched over a laptop at the London Business School, complaining that his shoulders hurt.

'Little did I know they were aching from carrying all those bags down Oxford Street,' I'd told Mr Mather-Lees.

The media had picked up on the soundbite and it had featured in the morning papers. Now, Ms Holland used it as an opportunity to try to undermine me by making it look like I was playing up to the media and enjoying being in the public eye.

'You seemed to find that funny,' she told me.

'I'm from the North-west of England,' I replied calmly. 'Life can be pretty hard. And the way we handle it is to make light of things when we can and make a joke.'

It surprised me that I felt able to take her on: previously I'd always held anyone in authority in high regard, but having gone through everything I had, I felt differently. I wasn't going to take my integrity being questioned.

Still, there was no doubt that the efforts of Alexander's defence team were emotionally pulverising. I knew it wasn't personal, but this wholesale trashing of my character left me feeling under siege.

At the same time, I knew that most people have an instinct for when you're telling the truth. As I stepped down from the witness box for the final time, it was with a sense that I had done everything I could. Now it was no longer down to me, but to the jury.

I didn't return to the court for another week, until the judge's summing up. During that time a number of people had been called to the witness box by the CPS, among them my ex-husband Clive, who spoke in support of me and also detailed his own limited interactions with Alexander, and my friend Venetia, who confirmed she had lent me money.

Tracey also gave lengthy evidence, and while I wasn't present for it, it made for fascinating reading when I finally got access to the transcript.

In her testimony, she said she had first met Alexander in 1989 and that from the start theirs had been an odd, largely nocturnal relationship, which she had tried to end on learning of his forthcoming fraud trial in Bournemouth relating to John Price, but he had then introduced her to his family, who had told her they believed he was wrongly accused.

Tracey had even lived with Philomena and Fred throughout Alexander's trial and had stuck by him through his eighteen-month prison sentence, following which he had been re-arrested and sent to Finland to serve another sentence for eighteen months.

When Alexander came out of prison, he had moved into a flat in Stroud with Tracey and Rosie, but Tracey told the court that while he had frequently asked her for money, Alexander had often stated that she wasn't rich enough for him.

The rest of her evidence was stuff she had already told me – that when she had discovered my pregnancy, he had told her I had forced him to have sex with me once, and that she had ended the relationship then but had later rekindled it because she felt 'duty bound' to be with him. As she had told me, she related how he had threatened to kill her with an axe if she left him.

For the first time, however, she also said that she knew he was meeting me with the sole object of getting money out of me, but that while she 'felt awful' about it, she was 'very depressed' and it was a 'difficult relationship'. 'Not as difficult as mine,' I couldn't help thinking. It felt like another terrible betrayal.

The other witnesses included DC Arkell, who detailed her own prolonged involvement in the case.

Finally, the prosecution case closed, and Alexander gave evidence in his own defence, which I won't allow him the dignity of featuring here.

Suffice it to say, it was all a pack of lies, with Alexander insisting that I had ruthlessly pursued him, and that he had never once asked me for money, but I had instead tried to buy his affections.

His lies unravelled under cross-examination, during which he repeatedly contradicted himself, something he then tried to blame on his failing memory when challenged by Mr Mathers-Lees.

'My memory is not good at the moment and hasn't been for two years,' he said.

He also claimed that while in Finland he had been 'taken by the Finnish Secret Service' and kept in custody for eleven weeks until his parents 'kicked up a fuss' and he was released. I had to smile at that.

Recalled by the defence the following day, Alexander continued to repeat his lies, insisting that he had 'made no false representations to Mrs Handy' and had never told me he was related to the Rothschild family.

'I cannot recall Christine Handy's portrayal of events, as they didn't happen,' he added.

It was ridiculous, and helpful to the prosecution, who felt that Alexander was damning himself with nearly every word he said.

Then, shortly before the judge's summing up, which marks the end of the submissions and evidence stage of a trial before it is handed over to the jury, Alexander's legal team announced that they had been sacked.

'We are no longer employed by Mr de Rothschild, and he would like to give his own version of events,' Ms Holland told the court. It made me laugh that they called him Mr de Rothschild, but technically they were right to do so: by this time he had changed his name by deed poll, to make the lie official.

That meant Alexander doing his own summing up, an excruciating ramble in which he continued to assert that I had told the court a pack of lies and that he was a victim of racial bias.

In some ways I wish I could have heard it: reading a court transcript later left me agog. I already knew the outcome by then, but it seemed to me that Alexander's inane ramblings and protestations had effectively hammered the final nail in his own coffin.

I knew the prosecution team felt the case had gone well, but nonetheless I was taking nothing for granted when, the following day, I returned to court and sat in the public gallery to observe the moment the jury were sent out to begin their deliberations.

Alexander, notably, wasn't there, having refused to come to court.

For the first time, I felt the return of my nerves. Did they believe me? I couldn't bear to think of the humiliation I might feel if this didn't go my way.

The jury was out for a nerve-racking three hours, although I would later learn that most of their verdicts had been decided incredibly quickly. Just one – on three counts relating to three separate payments of £500 that I had given Alexander to have my Jaeger clock returned from the jeweller, where he had sent it for repair – had proved troublesome.

My heart was in my mouth when the court usher brought the jury back in and the judge asked the foreman if they had reached a verdict on which they were all agreed.

'Yes, your honour,' he replied.

One by one the verdicts came in: a unanimous verdict of guilty. Seven in all out of the eight: I counted them on my fingers before the jury said that they couldn't come to a decision in relation to the Jaeger clock, the charges around which were of the least value and least interest to me – although I was pleased that the clock itself was returned to me after the trial. Those charges were left on file.

I am not one for open displays of emotion, but I wept with relief and pride. The jury had believed me. 'Thank you,' I mouthed down to them.

Of course, the case was not over quite yet, and if the jury thought they had heard some fairly extraordinary stuff in that austere courtroom, yet more was to come.

Turning to the jury, the judge, Julian Lambert, addressed them solemnly.

'You did not know that last year Mr de Rothschild was in court on seven charges of rape and molestation. We had a press ban on that so it couldn't influence your deliberations, but I have to sentence for that as well,' he told them.

I could see that the jury's eyes were on stalks with disgust as they tried to take in this unimaginable news.

I was pulled away from my miserable thoughts about what Alexander had done by the news that the judge would return to issue his sentence the next day. It meant another journey to and from court, but I was relieved – after the stress of the trial I was worried that I could not cope with a short prison term. I wanted the judge to throw the book at him.

And that is what he did. Alexander was given a fifteen-year sentence for what he had done to the underage girl, and three years for all seven counts of fraud, to run consecutively. That meant eighteen years in all.

I exhaled with relief, having been holding my breath once more. Justice had been served – and I had helped to make it happen. The authorities had recognised Alexander for the monster he was, and for that I was enormously grateful. Now I just had to try to get my money back.

21

THE AFTERMATH

It didn't take long for the euphoria of Alexander's conviction to dissipate. While it felt good to know he was now behind bars, a lot of the time I felt like I was serving a prison sentence of my own.

I wasn't the one in a cell, but there were many times in the years that followed his conviction where I envied him the knowledge that he had a roof over his head and food on the table, when often I didn't know where my next meal was coming from.

The reality was that, while justice had been served, it had done nothing to alleviate my desperate financial situation.

Of the £565,000 Alexander had stolen from me, I had managed to recover just under £50,000: £35,000 from the sale of the BMW, £12,000 raised from the goods I had brought back from the US, and £3,000 from the other goods discovered in the storage unit.

It barely scratched the surface of what I had lost.

A year after Alexander had been imprisoned, a Proceeds of Crime Act was made in my favour to the tune of £295,000, meaning I could make a claim on any money he had – but as he was incarcerated and without any assets that I could trace, it was unlikely I would receive any financial benefit.

One thing, meanwhile, had become abundantly clear: even casual scrutiny of the bank statements I'd had access to courtesy of Alexander's bankruptcy made it obvious that there had been negligence on a grand scale by two of our biggest high-street banks.

Of the money defrauded from me, £75,000 had passed through an account with the Royal Bank of Scotland, Cheltenham, and £352,000 through another bank, which I cannot name for legal reasons – and even a novice in such matters could see that both accounts had been woefully mishandled.

Alexander had opened one account – with the initial £75,000 banker's draft I had given him all the way back in 2003 – under an assumed name and with a fictitious address, which was only amended to the correct address several weeks later – by which time he had already withdrawn £40,000.

The bank seemed to have made no effort at all to check his identity or look at the source of the considerable funds that came into the account in lump transactions.

It was a similar tale with the other bank, which also appeared not to have made even basic checks on their new customer, opening an account for Alexander and accepting large deposits in the face of impaired credit, previous banking fraud, criminal convictions for theft and deception and recent prison sentences. This was the bank into which Alexander was also receiving Jobseekers' Allowance while simultaneously processing vast lump sums.

It seemed clear to me that the banks bore some responsibility for the money I'd lost – and I was determined to reclaim some of my lost funds from them.

I had no idea back then how exhausting it would be – four years of endless correspondence, being pushed from pillar to post as no one was prepared to take responsibility. At one point, one of the banks even threatened me with defamation proceedings after I set up a website to try to publicise what I was going through.

'Go ahead,' I told them. I would have liked nothing more than to see their treatment of me being brought out into the daylight.

Some people tried to help. My local MP was genuinely horrified when I attended his morning surgery and told him what I had been through. He contacted the Treasury on my behalf, and I had replies first from George Osborne's department and later from Sajid Javid, who was then Economic Secretary to the Treasury. Both said they sympathised with my plight.

It made no material difference, though. Months passed, then years, in which I was continually fobbed off, referred to first one banking official then another. Even with considerable pressure applied by Philip, weeks would go by before anyone bothered to respond to a letter, no matter how many times I chased it on the phone. When I could summon the energy to see the black humour in it all, I used to joke to Philip that if I was given ten pounds every time someone told me things were 'being looked into' then I would be wealthy enough to be able to drop my claim.

Either way, by November 2014, after nearly five years of correspondence, I took the decision to do something drastic to try to shine a light on what I had been subjected to.

'I'm going to walk from home to meet my MP at the House of Commons and then on to the bank headquarters in Canary Wharf,' I told Philip one night. It was a distance of 120 miles, and I gave myself ten days to do it.

Philip thought I was mad, as did my kids – but I was beyond caring what anyone thought by then. I just needed to do something, anything, to show that I wouldn't be defeated.

And that is what I did: for ten days I got up and walked, starting where I had left off the night before and trying to attract as much publicity as I could on the way. I went from Cheltenham to Cirencester, on to Fairford, Faringdon, Wantage, Reading, Twyford, Slough, Ealing Broadway and finally on to Parliament Square and Canary Wharf.

Each night, Philip would pick me up – I couldn't afford to stay overnight anywhere – and then drive me back again the next morning.

While I had initially hoped to drum up publicity to heap additional pressure on the banks, my worry about the effect on Marcus forced me to keep it low key. He was the only one of my children with a conman and rapist as a father, and I worried terribly about the legacy for him of his father's crimes. Even so, my mission wasn't without success: it spooked one of the banks into giving me the face-to-face appointment they had steadfastly avoided granting me so far.

They offered me a small sum by way of compensation. Again, it didn't remotely reflect the large sums of money – my money – that they had allowed to pass through the account; it was a 'shut up and go away' gesture really, but the reality was that by then I was so desperate that I didn't have much choice other than to accept.

I remember overhearing one of the senior members of the banking team talking about how much she was looking forward to flying to her holiday home for Christmas and thinking how I didn't even have a roof over my head to call my own.

The terrible reality was that by the time I came to do the walk, Marcus and I were homeless, shifting between one temporary accommodation and another. The downward spiral had begun in November 2011, when, back in Eldorado Road, I answered a knock on the door to two bailiffs issuing an eviction notice. It was a horrendous shock. I knew I was in arrears with my rent, but back then I was confident – perhaps foolishly – of getting some reparation from the banks and had tried to keep my landlady informed at every turn about what was going on.

To no avail: she wanted us out. On one level I couldn't blame her – this was her business, but it left me and Philip panic stricken. By then the landlady had applied for my bankruptcy, we had no money for a deposit and we had six kids between us.

On this occasion we got lucky, courtesy of a female friend who worked in a letting agency. After I rang her in tears, she told me she knew of a three-bedroom house near the racecourse in Cheltenham on Hill Court Road that was about to become available as the old lady who owned it was moving into a care home.

It hadn't been redecorated for some time, which meant the rent was cheaper than other equivalent properties in the area, although it still wouldn't be fully covered by housing benefit. In any case, it's not like I could afford to be choosy. My only sadness was having to say goodbye to Kabira, who had been so loyal. We helped her find new accommodation and a job, and we remain friends to this day.

In fact, the house was perfectly nice. Philip and I turned the dining room into a bedroom, which meant that Tom and Simon could share, while Sarah and Marcus each had a bedroom of their own. Philip's kids bunked down wherever they fancied when they came to stay.

If the children were upset at leaving Eldorado Road, they hid it well. Just as I had done during the turbulent preceding years, I tried to turn it all into a big adventure, and as they were still close enough to the town centre and to their friends, they didn't seem to mind.

I did everything I could to try to minimise the disruption to their lives: even when I was living hand to mouth they still had food in their tummies and clothes on their backs, while the fact that Clive was still paying their fees for private schools meant there was a seam of continuity in the background.

It didn't change the fact that I felt like I was endlessly fire-fighting. I got part-time jobs wherever I could to make ends meet, but the reality was that the demands of trying to juggle being a mum with the administrative hell of trying to get my money back meant I could only do minimum-wage jobs that barely made any difference to my mounting debts.

As the months went by it felt like one blow followed another. We'd only been in Hill Court Road for a year when the elderly lady's sons decided to sell the property.

That meant another move, this time to a bungalow on the outskirts of Cheltenham, which meant a three-mile walk for the kids to get into town.

By then I was also grieving my dad, who had passed away in March 2013 after a short illness, never able to see his youngest daughter get back on her feet. Both he and Mum had spent years desperately worrying about how I would get my money back. Now it was too late for Dad to see it.

It felt as though I would put one fire out, only for another to spring up in its place: after less than a year in the bungalow the landlord announced that he, too, would not be renewing the tenancy.

'It just feels like one step forward, two steps back,' I sobbed to Philip at the kitchen table after receiving the letter giving us notice.

This time I didn't have the strength to deal with this alone. I made an appointment with the housing department of the local council and told them that we were about to be made homeless.

Their solution was that Tom, Simon and Sarah would have to move in with their dad while they would put me and Marcus in bed-and-breakfast accommodation. Philip, mean-while, would have to make his own plans.

Philip wouldn't hear of it. 'Bed and breakfasts like the ones the council use are full of crackheads and criminals,' he said. 'There is no way I am seeing you in one of those.'

'What choice do I have, Philip?' I told him through yet more tears.

But Philip was nothing if not determined. At the end of September 2014, shortly before we had to vacate the bungalow, he told me he had scraped together enough money to pay for a week-long holiday let in the area.

'It's not long term, but it's something,' he told me.

It set the pattern that would unfold over the next six months: Philip would desperately beg and borrow the money for Marcus and I to move into temporary accommodation – usually holiday lets that were lying empty in-between seasons.

The moment we moved in we would have to start looking for somewhere else to live: sometimes I didn't even bother unpacking my suitcase. The longest I stayed in one place was three weeks.

On the weeks when we couldn't find anywhere – or simply didn't have the money to pay – I would have to take Marcus out of school and move in with my mum.

I wouldn't wish those six months on anybody. It was like a vicious spiral – with no address I wasn't able to claim benefits, and without benefits it was a struggle even to buy food to put on the table. I worried desperately about the toll on Marcus, being dragged from pillar to post, and on my elder kids, who were upset at being kept apart from their mum.

The worst thing was being unable to see a way out – and it was against that backdrop that I accepted a low five-figure sum from one of the banks in return for agreeing to drop any further action.

It wasn't nearly enough to make up for their negligence, but it was enough to give me and the children some security. We used £6,600 to pay upfront for a six-month rental of a house in Pittville Circus in Cheltenham town centre – no landlord would allow us to do otherwise because of our poor credit rating – which meant that with a new address we could apply for housing benefit once more.

The Royal Bank of Scotland never paid me a penny.

The permanent worry and stress about money, meanwhile, had started to leak into other areas of my life. Philip had been a rock throughout the fallout from my relationship with Alexander, but now the strain was starting to show on us too. There were lots of petty rows, and periods of silence, which in some ways were worse than the arguments. At least when we were arguing we were connecting with each other.

I knew we had to have a difficult conversation, but it was one that broke my heart to think about it. We had come so far together and gone through so much, but the reality was that we were both so battered by the events of the last few years that we just needed an escape from each other.

'This isn't working any more, is it?' I said one night as we sat side by side on the sofa, barely able to summon the energy to say a word to one another.

Beside me, Philip shook his head.

It was horrendously difficult for both of us to end it, even though I knew it was the right thing to do. I had grown so used to Philip being around that the thought of his absence terrified me. I worried about Marcus too. Philip had become like a father to him – Alexander had left by the time he was two, so Marcus didn't remember him. 'I know you're not my dad, but you're the only dad I have,' he would say to him on Father's Day, handing him the clumsily drawn card he had made at school.

Even so, I knew we couldn't go on as we were.

'It'll take time, but we will be friends again,' I told him on the day he moved out.

And we were. It wasn't easy, but we rebuilt a friendship from the ashes of our love affair, and I will always be grateful to him for the love and support he showed me during the most difficult part of my life.

Nonetheless, Philip's departure was devastating. I had prided myself on always remaining strong in front of the children, but on one occasion, not long after Philip had moved out, I was so overwhelmed that Marcus and Sarah came home from school to find me sobbing.

I can't even remember what had sent me over the edge. I just remember feeling like I was at the bottom of a deep, dark hole that I could never and would never get out of, no matter how hard I tried. All I know is that I'd never felt like that before, and that once I started sobbing I couldn't stop. I was so upset that my body was convulsing. To this day, I'll never forget the look on my daughter's face. She looked horrified.

Was I finally unravelling? I worried I might be. Once again, I rang the doctor, who suggested I try a course of antidepressants. I wasn't keen but took them as I figured I couldn't feel worse. It turns out I was wrong – they made me feel horrendous. It seemed that once again I would have to just pull myself up by my bootstraps and get on with it.

Around six months after Philip had moved out, another man unexpectedly came into my life. By then I was working in the coffee shop at the Cotswold Farm Park – owned by Adam Henson of BBC *Countryfile* fame – serving coffees to the ladies I used to lunch with when I was married to Clive. Adam was constructing a caravan park with a shower block, which meant a lot of workmen wanting a lot of tea and coffees.

Steve was often the one who came to collect them, and we would often share a joke whenever he came in. Then, a few weeks in, he slipped me a piece of paper with his number on.

'Give me a call and we'll go for a drink,' he said.

'Thanks, but I don't think so,' I replied. I liked Steve a lot, but I was still bruised from what had happened with Philip.

After a week or so, though, I decided a drink with someone who made me laugh was better than another night in front of the television. Sarah said she would look after Marcus, and Steve and I met for a drink.

One drink turned into another, then another. Steve was easy company, a straightforward bloke who was divorced with a daughter in her thirties called Yvonne and a granddaughter, Maddie, who was then thirteen, the same age as Marcus.

For the first time in a while, I felt the clouds lift. I hadn't belly-laughed in a long time, and it was refreshing to be around someone who wasn't embroiled in my complicated past.

It wasn't long before Steve and I were an item. Even so, we were flung unexpectedly closer together when, a few months after we met in February 2017, I learned that I had to be on the move once more: my landlord wanted to sell the house in Pittville Circus.

It was yet another demoralising episode. Property prices and rental prices had risen exponentially in the last year and my budget couldn't remotely cover another three-bedroom property in the centre of town. I looked at two-bedroom houses, figuring that, worst-case scenario, I could sleep on the sofa, but nothing I saw was suitable.

Again, I was despairing, but Steve had a solution. He, too, was looking for somewhere new to live, because although he owned a log cabin, complications with the land on which it was leased meant that he couldn't reside there permanently.

'Why don't we get somewhere together?' he suggested. It felt like a big jump to make as we'd only been together for six months, but it had to be worth a try.

Even then the only place we could afford was way out of town – a damp and gloomy ground-floor flat in a converted Cotswold manor house. It was cold, dark and remote, but it was affordable, even though it was a six-mile journey to Marcus's school.

The big downside was that Sarah, who was seventeen and still living at home, said she couldn't come with me. She was in her final year at college then, and the journey was just too much. It made more sense for her to live with her dad.

It broke my heart, taking me back to those miserable few months where I was trailing around holiday lets with Marcus. But I understood.

There was no getting away from the fact that it was a tough winter. By then Steve and I were both working for the same air-conditioning company, but when the owner died the business was wound up. We were surviving – just about – on universal credit. I was also worrying myself sick about Mum, whose health had taken a turn for the worse. My sisters were trying their best to be there for her, but it was becoming increasingly clear that she needed someone there on a permanent basis.

That's when Di suggested I move back home.

'Look, Christine, if things are that tough, why don't you come home and live with Mum?' she said.

I knew she was right, but it was hard not to feel defeated: while Garden City had many happy memories for me, I hadn't really expected to go back.

I told myself it wasn't going to be forever – although it didn't turn out that way.

The move to Flintshire in January 2019 was another upheaval, but most of all for Marcus, for whom it meant transferring to his third secondary school in as many years.

Life hadn't been easy for him on so many levels. As he got older, I had gently had to prepare him for the truth about the father who he resembles so closely in looks, although thankfully in no other way. There had been questions over the years about where his father was, and I had tried to answer them as honestly as I could without revealing too much of the devastating truth until I thought he was ready.

'He wasn't a very nice man,' I remember telling him as I gave him his tea one night, after he had returned from school asking why the other kids knew their real dads. For a while that seemed to satisfy him, but around the age of ten he started to go through a stage where he put Alexander on a pedestal.

'I often wonder what he's like,' he told me. 'And if I met him what he would think of me.'

It worried me as I know how manipulative Alexander is, and I knew there was a chance that he might try to contact Marcus once he was released from prison. Over time, I tried to emphasise that while we couldn't change the fact that Alexander was his father – and maybe he loved him in his own way – there was something about him that could never be trusted.

What hung over me most was the rape. It was bad enough to learn that your dad was a conman, but a sexual predator was far worse. Sometimes, I would lie awake at night running over conversations in my head, trying to rehearse how I would tell him.

As it happened the opportunity came up naturally. Marcus was around thirteen when, as we sat in the car on the way to do some errands, he mentioned that eighteen years seemed a long prison sentence for fraud.

'Most people do less than that even for bigger amounts of money,' he said. 'It's weird.'

I knew it was time. Pulling over in the car, I turned off the engine and took my son's hands in mine.

'It wasn't just fraud, Marcus,' I told him. 'He got three years for that, but he also got fifteen years for something even more horrible.'

The look that passed over his face as he took in the news was something I will never forget. He was repulsed and mortified.

'That's disgusting, Mum,' he told me, fighting back tears.

'If ever you want to talk about it, then you must always ask,' I told him.

In fact, he never has. But whatever latent feelings he might have had for Alexander de Rothschild – whose true parentage I never established, but who I can only assume was the biological son of Philomena and Peter Ariken, just like his siblings Lydia and Mason – were washed away that day. He calls him Marc Hatton – refusing to call him either Dad or even Alexander.

And whenever I look at my strong, loving, determined boy, I know he is the one part of my history that I would never change.

'We're a team, Mum, you and I,' he told me later that night. And we are.

EPILOGUE

Today

In May 2020 I received an email from the Victim Liaison department informing me that after two years on remand and a further ten years behind bars, Alexander had now served two-thirds of his sentence and had therefore reached the end of his prison term.

I had been told that as he had been born in Singapore he would almost certainly be deported back there at this point, but Alexander was still capable of making life difficult: he was fighting deportation and was subsequently being kept in prison on what is called an 'immigration hold'.

The uncertainty was unsettling. Months went by before, in January 2021, I learned that Alexander had been told he had a right to stay in the UK after all, because he had been adopted by Fred, a British citizen. The authorities had assumed he had Singaporean nationality like his mother Philomena, but this automatically gave him British citizenship. As ever, it seemed Alexander was still capable of throwing curve balls.

The news was broken to me this time in a phone call from a Victim Liaison Officer who explained the situation as gently as she could and was clearly sympathetic. Nonetheless, while I had half expected it, it was still a kick in the guts. For years I had taken some comfort from the fact that, come his release, Alexander would end up a continent and an ocean away – now he would be out there somewhere, less than 300 miles away from me in any direction.

There was nothing I could do. I didn't want to spend the rest of my life looking over my shoulder – Alexander had taken enough from me already.

He was eventually released on licence in February 2021. He is not allowed to contact me or Marcus, and at the point of writing I haven't heard from him. I do not know where he is and I have no right to know, although I was informed in a phone call on 20 December 2021 by my Victim Liaison Officer that he had asked for special permission to breach his licence. The permission was denied because of a very real risk that he could abscond.

Either way, I hope I never see him again, and that he does not lay waste to another woman's life as he did mine.

As for my life now … it's certainly not where I envisaged myself when I was younger, but I know I am lucky to have a roof over my head and food on the table.

I hadn't intended to settle in Garden City long term, but after Mum passed away in February 2019, taking over her home – with the blessing of my sisters – seemed like the sensible thing to do. It has given me some security for the first time in years.

Life still isn't easy. Between us, Steve and I have an array of health issues, which in my case means I can't stand or walk for a long time – although I'm still better off than Steve, who has all sorts of problems. I receive a carer's allowance for helping to look after him and that, plus income support, is what sees us through financially, although there is never any money left at the end of the month.

Money isn't everything, of course, and despite the challenges we are happy together, with an easy rapport that throws into sharp relief the superficial bubble that Alexander had created round me. We're both creative and have latterly found a great deal of pleasure pottering around salvage yards and home-clearance sales, finding bits and bobs we can transform or restore. We dream one day of buying a cottage in Wales and doing it up from scratch.

It's wonderful, too, that I have a great relationship with Steve's daughter, while he's great with my kids. Unexpectedly, we have built a new family together.

My family, of course, is the thing of which I am proudest of all: Alexander ruined a lot of things, but he didn't ruin that. My children are all doing well, we remain close, and they are happy.

Tom is now twenty-seven, and after taking a degree in animation, he works as a graphic designer and lives in Cheltenham with his girlfriend, Lizee.

My younger son Simon is now twenty-five. He studied for an undergraduate degree in fine art at Camberwell College of Arts and is now taking a master's degree in agriculture, forestry and food safety at Bangor University. He lives in wild and beautiful Snowdonia with his Welsh girlfriend, Gwen.

As for Sarah – she's now twenty-three and after graduating from her fine art degree in Manchester she ended up in Rotterdam, where she has her own pottery studio. She lives with her Dutch boyfriend, Thijs.

Last but not least, my youngest, Marcus, is studying for his A-levels, and hopes to join the RAF after school. I am so proud of them all, and what we have collectively achieved.

Bringing Alexander to justice took its toll, but if I could go back in time I would do it all again. Learning the truth behind the three and a half years we were together has helped me process what happened. In order to heal, I needed to know who he was, what he'd done and where my money was. I also wanted to stop him from doing what he had done to me to someone else: a leopard does not change its spots, and I have no doubt at all that, now he's out of prison, he will resort to his old pattern of fraud, exploitation and abuse.

Looking back, it amazes me that I managed it, given that at times it felt like everyone was against me. Reliving my experience through this book has reminded me how often I had to stare into the abyss – and pull myself back from it. But it has shown me something invaluable too. I may have lost a great deal, but I have found something too – that whatever life throws at me, I am a survivor.

ACKNOWLEDGEMENTS

Chrissy

My thanks to all those who have supported me over the last few years, particularly Robert and Eileen Buck, Tim Cash, Philip Price, Lekbira Karam, Diane and Steve Taylor, Charlie, Henry and Tilly and Leslie Rawlinson.

Huge gratitude and love to my children: Tom, Simon, Sarah and Marcus. And to Steve, for listening to endless hours of my psychobabble and drying my tears over a brandy. He's the cheapest therapist I've ever had! My thanks also to Kathryn for her patience and perseverance unravelling this story and for becoming such a good friend. It was a pleasure working with you.

Kathryn

My thanks go to my wonderful mum, Gwen, and late father, Jim. He would have been so proud that I'd finally written a book, even if the story was not my own. I owe huge gratitude to my lovely husband and daughter, Duncan and Connie, for putting up with all my book-related stress, and a very big thank you to all the friends who have supported me along the way too – you know who you are. Finally, my immense thanks to Chrissy for trusting me to tell her extraordinary story. I've no doubt we are friends for life!